# PRAIS

## CRAIG GROSS

## AND *GO SMALL*

"Craig's book couldn't have come at a better time. In a whirlwind of everyone being about platforms, analytics, and growth, Craig reminds us of the upside-down economics of the Kingdom of God. How different the world would be if Christians gave every ounce of energy to being faithful to what God has already given them, and *Go Small*."

— Jefferson Bethke, author,
*Jesus > Religion*

"Everywhere we look there's pressure to go big and ignore the small stuff. Craig's new book is a refreshing call to focus on what God has put in front of you, despite the size of its impact. Jesus told us to be faithful in the small things and this book is a much needed reminder that God is in the details, big and small."

— Kyle Chowning, entrepreneur

"Craig does what he does best: state sublimely profound truths."

— Propoganda, spoken-word artist
and rapper

"In *Go Small*, Craig Gross tells the church to wake up and notice the Divine that is in all, through all, and above all - the Spirit that permeates everything, if only we have the eyes to see and the ears to hear."

— Seth Taylor, author, *Feels Like
Redemption*

# PRAISE FOR *OPEN*

"I like Craig Gross because he keeps it real—no fake shallow stuff with him. He has a deep passion to see people experience freedom, and in *Open*, he will help you find the freedom you've been searching for."

— Derwin L. Gray, lead pastor,
Transformation Church; author,
*Limitless Life*

"*Open* is one of the most relative and practical books on accountability I've ever read. Craig takes many routes, through stories from pop culture and his personal journey to help lead you to a life that's *open*."

— Josh McCown, Tampa Bay
Buccaneers quarterback

"Craig Gross occupies a very, very important space in the Christian community and the culture at large. He calls men and women to not just fight addictive problems but gives them the tools, encouragement and community they need to actually get free and live free. But living free requires being *open* with your life, and Craig's incredible book is both a clarion call to always live in the light and simple instruction guide for how to ensure you stay there."

— Shaunti Feldhahn, social
researcher; best-selling author,
*For Women Only* and *For Men
Only*

"Craig has been a friend and ministry partner for years. He has always been as helpful and hopeful as he is honest. This book comes to you in that spirit."

— Ryan Meeks, founding pastor,
EastLake Church

"I don't say this often, but this book is a must-read. Every time I speak somewhere or get emails with people asking me how to find healing in particular areas, my response is always *community*. Craig does a beautiful job in articulating how the path to true joy is found in being real, honest, and accountable."

— Jefferson Bethke, author,
*Jesus > Religion*

"This book will challenge you. And with good reason, because isn't that inherent to accountability? In a culture that grows increasingly autonomous, it is essential that we pursue one another with intentionality. From a man that has been blessed by the ministry of XXXChurch and the Gross family, I am thankful for Craig—his heart for and devotion to life lived together. I pray that this book will serve as a practical guide for openness and intimacy that reflects the communal nature of our Creator."

— Levi (the Poet) Macallister,
spoken word and performance
artist

"In a time when many of us communicate through quick, abbreviated texts, and social media lends itself to the proclamation of 'truth' through a series of monologues, Craig Gross reminds us that life is about authentic relationships; relationships that seek truth through *true accountability!*"

— Michael Guido, road pastor, PR
Ministries

"*Open* by Craig Gross gives us a simple yet fresh look at what it really takes to overcome the many things that can consume us and can keep us from experiencing sustainable freedom through Christ and community. This book is a true road map to living life openly, honestly and with genuine courage."

— Judah Smith, pastor, City
Church; *New York Times* best-
selling author, *Jesus Is _____*

# GO SMALL

# GO SMALL

### Because God Doesn't Care About Your Status, Size, or Success

## CRAIG GROSS

### with Adam Palmer

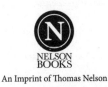

NELSON
BOOKS

An Imprint of Thomas Nelson

Published in Nashville, Tennessee, by Nelson Books, an imprint of Thomas Nelson. Nelson Books and Thomas Nelson are registered trademarks of HarperCollins Christian Publishing, Inc.

Thomas Nelson, Inc., titles may be purchased in bulk for educational, business, fund-raising, or sales promotional use. For information, please e-mail SpecialMarkets@ThomasNelson.com.

Unless otherwise noted, Scriptures are taken from the Holy Bible, New International Version®, NIV®. Copyright © 1973, 1978, 1984, 2011 by Biblica, Inc.™ Used by permission of Zondervan. All rights reserved worldwide. www.zondervan.com.

Scriptures marked NKJV are from THE NEW KING JAMES VERSION. © 1982 by Thomas Nelson, Inc. Used by permission. All rights reserved.

**The Library of Congress Cataloging-in-Publication
Data is on file with the Library of Congress**

ISBN: 978-1-4002-0532-5

*Printed in the United States of America*

14 15 16 17 18 19 RRD 6 5 4 3 2 1

I wanted to dedicate this book to three people
who have inspired me to go small.

Jeanette, thank you for always being willing to do the work
for the ministry that oftentimes I even overlook. I couldn't
do this without you, nor would I want to. I owe you several
more dedications for the wife role you play in my life.

Michelle Truax, thanks for being on this roller coaster with me
for ten years. Your contributions to this ministry on a daily
basis behind the scenes have been an amazing blessing.
Here's to the next ten! Gosh—you'll be really old then.

Adam Palmer, thanks for the motivation for this project and for
being the guy behind the computer making me sound like I can
spell and talk in complete sentences, and for adding your voice
to these conversations. Thanks for encouraging me to go small!

# CONTENTS

# Part 3: How to Go Small

# FOREWORD

Go small.

Say it out loud.

Really loud, like you're excited.

Sounds funny, huh? That's because we are so pre-disposed to the notion that bigger is better. This never became more clear to me than when I reached one of my childhood dreams of becoming an NFL player. Well, maybe my dream wasn't exactly fulfilled, because my dream was to get drafted by the Dallas Cowboys and lead them to multiple Super Bowls, all while having some great, transcendent spiritual impact on all those who watched me thank God as I received the MVP trophy.

Realistically, my career has been far from that, but it has been thirteen years of professional football, including stops in the now defunct UFL, with eight different NFL teams and countless teammates. It's been fun, but not the dream scenario I thought God had mapped out for me.

There was, however, a small moment along that journey

when my focus changed. It happened in year nine, when the phone stopped ringing and teams were no longer eager to sign me. I had to make a choice.

That's when I went small. Or maybe my circumstances led me to go small. Regardless, I finally stopped fighting the very thing God was trying to show me would bring me the greatest joy.

Out of work and possibly transitioning into life after football, I began looking for things to do and ended up coaching at our local high school, mostly to fill time, but also as an opportunity to stay around the game of football. However, as I got to know the team, the players, and the coaches, I realized these young men were real people with real stories, just like the people in any NFL locker room. They were no different, and their lives were just as important.

I poured my heart and soul into coaching those kids, and as a result, I began to feel a joy I hadn't felt on a football field in a long time. It was crazy: I'd played in the NFL, started a few games, and thrown touchdowns to future Hall-of-Famers, and yet I found my greatest joy on the practice field in Waxhaw, North Carolina. Why? Because I was internalizing something I had known to be true but never fully grasped.

I was going small.

None of it made sense. We weren't on TV and we didn't have five-star recruits—we were just a plain ol' ordinary high school football team. Yet I felt so much peace and fulfillment. I developed relationships with those players that I will carry with me for the rest of my life, but it wasn't because I played in the NFL. Sure, that's cool to high school kids, but it wears off eventually. No, we connected because, for that season, I took a genuine interest in their lives. I can recall one player saying, "Coach, I appreciate you; not because of what you've taught me about football or that you played in the NFL, but because you asked me how my day went."

Four small words, one small sentence—"How was your day?"—and yet it meant so much.

I finished that season with those kids and ended up getting a call from the Chicago Bears. With my focus shifted on the small, I went into my new job wanting to serve every teammate I could, wanting to focus on every person in the building. It's amazing what kind of peace and fulfillment you get from serving others, it's almost as if God knows you will be at your best when you're not focused on yourself.

I was signed as a backup quarterback by the Bears, which means that, in 2013, when the starting quarterback was injured, my number was called and I got a chance to step in. The games I was able to play afforded me an opportunity to compete to be a starting quarterback once more, this time for the Tampa Bay Buccaneers. We'll see what happens on the field but off the field I plan to go in with the same approach I had in Chicago.

During the off-season, my friend Craig handed me this

book, *Go Small*, and I believe it will give you the encouragement you need to free you up from the grandeur of chasing number-based success and allow you to find your true purpose, right where God has you! Don't be too big to read *Go Small*. For every person caught in the gap of success and significance, this book can be life-changing.

—Josh McCown
Quarterback, Tampa
Bay Buccaneers

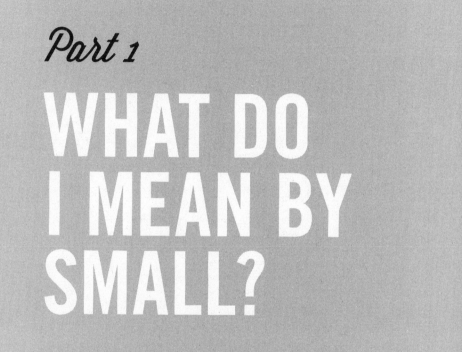

*Part 1*

# WHAT DO I MEAN BY SMALL?

*Chapter 1*

## GO BIG OR GO HOME

The Golden Gate Bridge, connecting the city of San Francisco with Marin County by spanning the Golden Gate Strait, is one of our world's most recognizable landmarks. Its red, wiry structure is a remarkable symbol of connectivity, of the feats that humans can achieve through collaboration and intelligence.

It's also the second-most popular destination in the world for people to kill themselves.

Roughly once every two weeks, a person caught in a dark web of isolation, depression, and hopelessness chooses to climb over the protective guardrails and jump, plummeting a total of 250 feet down, down, down into the cold waters of the strait. When they reach the bottom, they're traveling roughly seventy-five miles per hour. Most people die upon impact.

There was a suicide note collected a few years ago that was written by an anonymous person as they made their way to the Golden Gate Bridge. The writer remarked that they were walking to the bridge with the intent of ending their life; but one sentence of the note immediately leapt out at me.

"If one person smiles at me on the way," this person wrote, "I will not jump."

They jumped.

Suicide affects men and women of all ages and races, and since it is an ultimate choice, it is not something that anyone embarks upon lightly. The person who wrote this heartbreaking and tragic note hadn't decided on the spur of the moment that life was no longer worth living, and likely they had people in their world—family, friends, coworkers—who may have been able to provide the hope or welcoming arms that they were obviously missing. It's also worth remarking on the very real possibility that this person wouldn't have been able to recognize a hopeful smile if anyone *had* given them one.

But what if someone had?

What if, as this tormented person made their solemn way to the Golden Gate Bridge, some stranger had seen them—really *seen* them—and offered the smallest, simplest gift we can offer another human being?

Is it possible that something as simple as a smile can save a life?

---

In many ways this book is a reaction. To what, exactly? Partly, it's a reaction to the not-so-subtle and ultimately insidious message our culture seems to send us nonstop: "Go big or go home."

If you aren't going to swing for the fences, you might as well not even step up to the plate.

If you won't sign off on every last letter and punctuation mark of my political manifesto, then you aren't a true patriot.

If you aren't eating a gluten-free, vegan diet by now, then you might as well buy a lifetime supply of Chicken McNuggets, because you obviously hate your children.

Relax, people.

But before you nod your head knowingly, thinking you've already figured out where this book is going, let me add something more to the mix: this book is *also* a reaction to a subtle message we receive through the second half of the motto I quoted above—the "go home" part. There are many, many, many people who *try* to "go big" and don't make it happen, so they give up.

They go home.

They quit. They resign themselves to a desperate, futile life of punching a time clock at work before heading to a night in front of their TVs—or worse, their smartphones. They settle for putting their heads down and just getting by for the next few decades until their time on earth has passed and they fade away to join millions—billions—of quietly desperate souls who have gone before them.

Maybe you feel like that. Maybe you feel exhausted from doing nothing, having tried repeatedly to go big. Or maybe your pendulum has swung the other way and now you've basically given up on doing *anything* worthwhile and have gone home.

Maybe you feel a constant, ever-present sort of disappointment because no matter how big you go, no matter how radical you try to be in your endeavors, it's just never enough. Maybe you've done some really cool and huge things—things that make the world a better place or that look really great as bullet points in a fund-raising newsletter—but you still feel like you could be doing more.

Either way, wherever you are on the spectrum, I want to give you permission to breathe. To relax. To find contentment instead of comfort.

I want to show you the miraculous world of the ordinary. Of the little things.

Of the small.

One thing people in both Western and Eastern civilizations, from country to country all around the world, seem to love right now are superhero stories. Especially when it comes to movies. There's just something about heading to the movie theater or cranking up the Blu-ray player and watching men and women with special, unique abilities punch the stuffing out of one another and kick up a lot of dust and collateral damage in the process.

We love it. Batman, Iron Man, Thor, Superman, Spider-Man, Captain America . . . the list goes on. The background narrative almost always seen in these films, the one we keep watching over and over, is that of an ordinary person rising above the rabble and doing something extraordinary—usually because they have to protect a person, town, country, or planet against some malevolent or maniacal evil force. Aliens or Nazis or some rich guy with a tragic backstory who is intent upon watching the world burn while cackling in the firelight.

But one consistent thing about most (if not all) superhero stories is the format, usually beginning with what is known in the storytelling business as an *origin story.* This is usually the first film in the new or "rebooted" franchise, when they start over with a new actor taking on the role of the superhero after the original actor got too old or started demanding too much money.

The origin story is the way we as viewers learn how our heroes became heroes in the first place, the origin of particular characters. How Peter Parker got bitten by a radioactive spider—or genetically modified spider, depending on the film (or comic book)—and how that changed him from the inside out. How Bruce Wayne became a vigilante who turned his childhood fear of bats into motivation to avenge his parents' murders. How Thor, uh, used a rainbow bridge to come to earth and became an Avenger . . . Okay, maybe that's not the best example.

Anyway, one thing you may notice when watching these superhero origin stories is the formula. You have a few minutes at the beginning of the film when our not-yet-a-hero is some ordinary person, probably getting beat up or whatever. Then some accident happens in a lab or they discover they've been a mutant all along, and with that accident or discovery comes the realization that something fundamental has shifted: they're now an extraordinary being in an ordinary world.

And then they fight somebody or something, and then the movie's over.

But there is a crucial part of this superhero origin story that we seldom see play out in anything more than a scene or two: the training.

Usually superhero training is handled in what is known as a montage. You know what this is: some cool song plays on the soundtrack while we see our newly minted hero trying out this or that superpower. Peter Parker covers his room with spiderwebs. Bruce Wayne pummels things in the mountains of Nepal. Tony Stark fires up a blacksmithing bellows in prison and hammers stuff. The point is, the movie is telling us, "So, the hero is learning things, and we know it's boring so we're going to give you the idea that this is happening then quickly skip to the interesting part. Just hang with us and we'll get back to the explosions and punching soon, okay?"

I agree. The training *is* boring.

But also, *the training is everything.*

Nothing happens without the training. Without the training our hero is just a person with a bunch of cool powers he doesn't know how to harness. Without the training the world isn't saved and the bad guys aren't thwarted. Without the training the woman in peril isn't saved—and it's almost *always* a woman in peril (don't get me started on that).

Without the training we don't have a story—instead, we have a hero who gets squashed with hardly a thought on the villain's way to total victory.

So these filmmakers and storytellers include the training, but they skip past it as quickly as possible. And once you start to notice this training-skipping, you'll see it everywhere, and not just in superhero tales.

For example, it also happens in romantic comedies. The harried young career woman (really—are there *that* many women working for magazines or in advertising?) just can't seem to find the right man. Maybe she's too career-oriented or keeps dating doofuses, but she is always unlucky in love. Then she meets a handsome stranger in some cute, out-of-the-blue way—they run into each other on the sidewalk and drop their groceries! they argue over a taxicab! they collide while ice-skating in rural Alaska!—and they wind up going on a date or something, and over the course of the film, they fall in love.

Except we don't see that part, right? We see a dating montage—again, up comes the jaunty pop song on the soundtrack, then we're treated to various shots of our star-crossed couple at the county fair eating cotton candy, or laughing and holding hands as they walk out of a movie, or contemplating a field of stars while sitting on a picnic blanket.

Romantic comedies love to tell the story of two people

meeting and falling in love. But the actual falling-in-love part? That's boring. In real life, love is made up of a bunch of quiet moments, of small steps together that don't appear to cover much ground. Love is something we often don't even recognize until we've been in it for a while. The *feeling* of being in love is great! But the actual *making* of a long-term relationship? That's pretty ordinary and small. So let's just cover it in a montage.

Or take sports, for example, where we tend only to hear about training in the context of a big championship event like the Super Bowl or the Olympics. Professional athletes by and large have spent much of their lives training, training, training for that big moment. The wide receiver who drops a last-second touchdown pass in the Super Bowl has caught that same pass probably tens of thousands of times in practice and in all the games leading up to that moment—in Pop Warner football, in junior varsity, in high school, in college, in the Arena Football League, on the practice squad, and in every NFL game before then.

Athletes practice a lot, and when they're finished, they practice some more. They spend hours and hours of every day practicing—often to the detriment of any sort of a social life—until everything becomes rote. And even then, they keep practicing. It's all so very, very ordinary and small.

But it's *necessary*. In the big moments you as a fan are going to be grateful for the countless hours of work the offensive tackle put in on the practice field and in the film room, because he recognizes a specific defensive blitz package and is able to prevent the defense from getting to the quarterback, who is able to spot the open receiver and throw the winning touchdown pass.

Without training, without the hours and hours and hours of tumbling and turning cartwheels, the young gymnast can have a little trip-up in her Olympic free routine and go from a gold-medal performance to missing the podium entirely.

As a rule, people generally don't make movies about training. It isn't interesting from a storytelling perspective, and it won't sell millions of dollars' worth of tickets.

But without it nothing great happens.

In fact, it's *during* the training montage when the greatness is *built.* The big game or the climactic battle sequence or the twenty-fifth wedding anniversary simply reveals the greatness forged in those long, dreary, small, ordinary hours in between big moments.

The ordinary, small times mean something.

In some respects they mean *everything.*

It is in the seemingly ordinary moments of life when God does His greatest work.

And *that's* what this book is about.

---

I grew up in California, where you pretty much have to drive wherever you want to go, and since I still live here, I don't know a whole lot about mass transportation in more compact cities like New York City, Boston, or Chicago. But

I do know about a man named Clive Jacobsen, and I also know a little bit about how he uses his time on a train that runs from his house in Sydney, Australia, to a town called Shellharbour.

Every Sunday Clive Jacobsen gets on the train with a leather duffel bag, finds a comfortable seat, and settles in for the four-hour journey. He isn't going to pass the time looking at the scenery out the window, though. Nor will he strike up any conversations with his fellow passengers, read the latest paperback thriller, or scroll through his Twitter feed on a smartphone.

Clive Jacobsen will unzip his duffel bag, get out a note-pad and a pen, and start writing letters.

The letters he writes will eventually find their way to distant countries like Zambia, South Africa, or Thailand.

Clive Jacobsen is writing to international prisoners.

Criminals.

He writes to inmates because he was one once. Long ago. Back in the mid-1960s, Clive Jacobsen spent a small amount of time in jail for a relatively minor offense, but he's never forgotten the sense of isolation and abandonment he felt while he was there. So it seemed only natural that when a letter-writing organization contacted him in 2002 about sending letters to inmates abroad, he seized the opportunity right away.

The organization told him he could write to more than one inmate if he liked, so he decided to write to three. As his correspondence went on and he began to develop relationships—however distant—with these men, he began not only to see the massive need for this type of pen pal but also to find some personal fulfillment through it. So he upped it to four.

Then ten. Then twenty. Then a hundred.

At last count, Clive Jacobsen now maintains written correspondence with more than 550 prisoners abroad.

That is a lot of time on the train.

Clive not only sacrifices his time and invites the pain of inevitable hand cramps from handwriting all those letters; he also sacrifices his money. According to Clive, he can spend as much as $200 every month on postage alone, in addition to all the other supplies he uses to organize his correspondence.

This guy is an amazing example for all of us because he's just doing what God put in front of him. He saw an opportunity to reach out to some of the most marginalized and isolated people in the world and shine a light on them to let them know that no matter what they've done, Jesus still loves them and somebody sees them.

As far as the people Clive writes to, many of them were caught for minor offenses like stealing food, and a majority of the letters he writes are to men who were attempting to help their families in some way. They live in countries with extreme poverty and no opportunities to get out of it; many of them, in a fit of desperation, did something criminal in an effort to take care of their kids or wives.

They land in prison and are sentenced to lengthy stays,

and their families—the very people they were trying to help—abandon them.

Clive Jacobsen understands this about them, and his heart goes out to them. In his words, "They can't undo the crime they've done . . . but no one is beyond redemption."

And if you think what Clive Jacobsen is doing does nothing for *him*, then I would suggest you haven't thought through this very much. I would imagine that something as small and simple as writing letters to these inmates helps Clive Jacobsen understand his own need for redemption—and reinforces to him how much Jesus has done for him.

He isn't trying to change the world. He's just trying to bring a little peace into these men's lives, and in so doing he brings some peace into his own.

And he does it by thinking small.

Go big or go home? That's a false choice.

I encourage you to pull a Clive Jacobsen and go small.

*Chapter 2*

# RIGHT HEART, WRONG PLACE

You ever heard of a guy named Naaman? We read about this dude in the book of Judges in the Old Testament, and we can learn a thing or two from his story.

Naaman was a soldier for the army of Syria—and a good one too—who had a disease called leprosy. In case you don't know, the type of leprosy mentioned in Scripture was a particularly disgusting, highly contagious skin disease that carried a lot of negative connotations in the Middle Eastern world of the Bible. Bottom line was: if you had leprosy, you were in a bad, bad way both in terms of your health and in terms of your standing in the world.

So here was Naaman, a decorated and respected soldier, and the poor guy had it. Leprosy.

Oh, yeah: in addition to leprosy, Naaman had a young Israeli girl whom he'd taken captive after a successful military campaign and brought all the way home to Syria, putting her to work in his house as a servant for his wife. This young girl, hearing about Naaman's affliction, casually mentioned that he should seek out a prophet from her home country of Israel, a guy named Elisha.

Now Elisha was a very well-known prophet in Israel, mainly because he had a seemingly direct connection with God. The man did a ton of miracles in God's name, raising people from the dead, providing them with financial resources, turning poisonous food into something wholesome for a whole group of other prophets—and that's just in one chapter of the Old Testament book of 2 Kings.

The point is, Elisha was a powerful dude.

Because of Elisha's power and reputation, it's safe to assume Naaman had already heard of him and the amazing things he was able to do in God's name. So Naaman decided to take this slave girl's advice to heart and journey to Israel to seek out Elisha. It wasn't a short trip—not like driving down to see the prophet on the corner, or like going to fill up your car with gas or heading over to the grocery store really quickly to pick up some bread to go with dinner.

No, this was a major road trip requiring some serious planning, major resources, and a whole lot of time. He also brought, literally, a half ton of silver and gold, as well as some fancy garments he hoped to use as payment for being cured—garments were an acceptable form of payment back then, apparently. Naaman was going all-in with this getting-rid-of--leprosy stuff. In fact he even took a note from his king, the king of Syria (some Bible translations use "Aram" instead of "Syria," by the way), to give to the king of Israel, letting him know what was up and why Naaman has come to Israel.

Naaman showed up in Israel ready to go. He'd made the probably weeks-long journey; he was loaded down with precious metals; he'd spoken to kings about his condition—the man was obviously expecting something special. He had all he needed to make a big splash, impress the stuffing out of this prophet, and buy his health.

Except it didn't really happen that way.

Not at all.

Here's what *did* happen. Naaman showed up in Israel and headed toward Elisha's house, but before he could even get there, Elisha sent a messenger to meet him in the street. The messenger stopped Naaman's caravan and gave him a message from Elisha, saying, and I'll paraphrase here: "I know why you're coming to see me, and you don't need to come any farther. Just go to the Jordan River, wash yourself in it seven times, and then you'll be back to normal and your leprosy will be gone."

Just like that.

Sounds easy enough, right? But that very aspect of it—that it sounds easy—rubbed Naaman the wrong way. He couldn't believe the audacity of this Israeli prophet! He was sure this great man of God would come out and *do* something to make the leprosy go away, that he would recite some incantation or perform some ritual bit of hand-waving that would result in a cure. But no! Elisha wanted him to dunk himself in a river.

And not only that—the river in question was the *Jordan*. Naaman, for whatever reason, bristled at the thought. If it were only a matter of washing in a river, Naaman would have rather done it in one of the rivers in his home country. In his mind, after all, they were better than any rivers in dirty old Israel.

Now I'm sure there are some ancient political and social aspects that are lost on us in modern times. That's not the point, though, and it's not why I'm telling you this story. What I really want to get to is something Naaman's servant said to him, which we can read in 2 Kings 5:13. He told Naaman, "If the prophet had told you to do some great thing, would you not have done it? How much more, then, when he tells you, 'Wash and be cleansed'!"

Regardless of any social or political dynamics, the actual *thing* Elisha told Naaman to do—dip himself in a river seven times—was pretty darn easy. Pretty simple.

Pretty small.

But Naaman had to be convinced that it was worth his time. He was too busy expecting the big show to realize that he had perfect health in his grasp.

It wasn't a matter of submitting to God. If you think about it, Naaman was already willing to sell out his own gods in order to bring about his healing. He surely had some idols back home in Damascus who would be none too pleased to find out he was off in Israel, looking for a prophet that served Israel's God, in order to be cured.

So no, Naaman mostly had his heart in the right place.

He just had his sights set on the wrong one.

He was hoping for the fireworks, for the laser-light

show, for the all-out, sparkly, complete-with-a-rock-and-roll-soundtrack *healing*.

Of course if you don't already know the story, you can probably figure out what happened. He listened to his servant's good advice, took a quick jaunt down to the Jordan River, dipped himself in the water seven times, and came out completely restored.

Just like that.

God gave him an ordinary job and turned it into something extraordinary.

I am convinced that deep down—or maybe not so deep down—most of us can empathize with Naaman. We want to see something *big* happen in our lives, because if something big happens, it feels like proof that it was important. That we were worth the trouble. That we've accomplished something.

More often than not, however, we *don't* see those big things happening. Because, honestly, how often can big things happen?

Think about your own life. How many legitimately extraordinary things have happened to you? How many have you accomplished? How many truly transcendent meals have you had versus the number of times you simply ate in order to solve the calorie problem for that day? How many hours have you slogged through the workday versus the number of hours you've come alive at the goals you've accomplished? And I say that as a person who heads up a nonprofit organization, who does what he loves. Even

I have mostly bland, ordinary days with a few high spots peppered in.

No, the big things are few and far between. That's what makes them big.

---

I don't know if you're familiar with the concept of New Monasticism, but it's a fairly recent resurgence in communal living—sort of a modern, updated version of living in a monastery or convent, but without all the separation from society. It's generally a bunch of good-hearted Christian believers living together in the same house with a strong spiritual intentionality. These people generally have a rhythm of communal and individual prayer, Scripture reading, meals, and community service, among other things.

One such community was fairly well known in the new monastic movement. How, exactly, they became well known is a story I do not claim to know or understand, but they famously posted a sign on one of their walls that very succinctly sums up all I've just been talking about. It read:

"Everyone wants a revolution. No one wants to do the dishes."

A revolution? That's the type of big thing people like me—and maybe even you—are looking for, are trying to bring about. We're hoping for a revolution of God's love and grace to envelop the world with the wonderful message of Jesus' sacrifice and redemption. That a better, more fulfilling, more peaceful and wonderful life awaits those who would give it over to the Lord.

That's the big idea behind what we do at XXXchurch .com, and it's the big idea behind countless other nonprofit, church, and parachurch organizations.

We all want revolution.

But boy, we do *not* want to do the dishes.

The boring, bland, everyday tasks and chores, the foundational material of just living life? That stuff is so far away from the excitement of the revolution that it almost feels like a step backward to do it.

But it's necessary. And it's good.

It's part of the revolution. The three-times-daily work of doing the dishes to make sure everything is clean and orderly at mealtime. To ensure no one gets sick from eating off dirty plates. To develop the discipline of routine and organization.

Doing the dishes—the ordinary, small stuff—is the raw material that the revolution is built out of. Without someone doing the dishes, you wouldn't have a revolution in the first place.

That's why we have to think small. That's why we have to put our hearts in the right place.

---

I'd like to tell you about my friend Rachel. XXXchurch .com helps people who use pornography clean up their lives and quit, and simultaneously also helps people who *make* pornography—either in front of or behind the camera—get out of the industry if they so desire. When we started XXXchurch.com in 2002, the very first thing we did to announce our organization to the world was to buy booth space at a pornography trade show.

Yes, there are pornography trade shows.

Anyway, we figured Jesus was always into rolling up His sleeves and getting down and dirty, meeting the lost people wherever they happened to be in the midst of their lost-ness, so a porn show would be the perfect place for us to go. Ever since that first show, we realized how necessary this type of outreach was, and we've continued to go back to that original show—and to several others—every year.

So what do we do when we minister at these porn shows? Do we do something outlandish and extravagant and extraordinary? Not really. Our approach is simple—we have Bibles with the phrase "Jesus Loves Porn Stars" emblazoned on the cover, and we hand those out to whomever. Then we just talk to people. We find out about them, about their stories, about how they came to be at the porn show, and that's about it. There's a lot of relational conversation and not a whole lot of hellfire and brimstone preaching. By "not a whole lot," I mean "none at all, dear Lord, why would we do that?"

We're in an extraordinary environment, but when you get to the core of it, what we're doing is pretty ordinary.

Now that you have some background and context, let me tell you about my friend Rachel, who has been going to these porn shows with us almost since the beginning. Rachel is one of the best people to handle this environment for a lot of reasons, but here are the two best: nothing fazes her, and she can talk to anyone. She smiles all the time, and it's a genuinely happy smile, not the fake, toothy grin of the politician or watered-down pastor. Rachel is a fountain of optimism, even in the midst of a spiritually grimy place like a porn show.

Rachel has been doing this for years, and it's always the same. She hands out Bibles, strikes up conversations, gets genuinely interested in people, and takes it from there. Since Rachel goes with us to the same shows year after year, she often sees the same people over and over again, and one of those people was a porn actress who went by the stage name Jenna, but whose real name is Brittni. They would encounter each other almost every year at this one specific show, and they would always have a good conversation about normal things, about Jesus, about whatever Brittni wanted to talk about, really, which was usually not porn.

You know: ordinary stuff.

Or as Brittni called it, girl talk.

This went on for *seven years*, until we received an e-mail, to Rachel from Brittni, in the general in-box at XXXchurch. With Brittni's permission, I'd like to show it to you here:

My name is Brittni. I used to be an adult "star." I met Rachel several times at the Exxxotica conventions. I would stop by the XXXchurch booth to see her—she is so beautiful, I absolutely love and adore her. I want to give her the most amazing praise report. Thank you, Jesus, I found him. I am home!

It has been a long seven-year journey of porn, prostitution, stripping, drugs, alcohol, and several failed suicide attempts. But I made it! Little did I ever know I would stumble upon XXXchurch again since leaving the adult industry. Well you guys found me, or I found you, or it is simply in God's plan. [A friend] stumbled across your magazine in our pastor's office and passed it on to me. I could not believe my eyes when I realized, "Wow! These are the 'Jesus Loves Porn Stars' people!" Then I saw Rachel's picture and I just had to let her know that I am saved!

I want to thank her for all of her kind words and loving spirit. I don't know if she realizes how she impacted me or not, but her being so kind and nonjudgmental always felt so good. I never felt love in my life and was looking for it in all the wrong places. It felt great to speak to [a] woman as beautiful as Rachel who would tell me I was her favorite and just have normal, nonporn, girl talk.

Please tell her that I thank her from the bottom of my heart and I will never forget what she has done for me. I will be attending the seminar in September and I cannot wait to see her in a completely different light. I have finally encountered the unconditional love of God and I will never go back.

Pretty amazing, right?

After Brittni contacted us, we got in touch with her and she told us, "I saw Rachel and she always told me I was beautiful, and she always smiled, and always talked to me."

How ordinary is that? There is nothing extreme or radical about a woman smiling at another woman and complimenting her looks. For someone like Rachel, that sort of behavior comes as naturally to her as breathing. That's just who Rachel *is*.

But what if Rachel had her heart in the wrong place? What if she took the vantage point that a lot of us—especially in the church world—take, where we have to quantify our results and make sure we're "planting our seed in good soil," as some people like to say? What if Rachel decided all the time, energy, and resources she was expending over the course of *seven years* weren't worth it? What if Rachel got burned out during that sixth year and decided she wasn't going to do outreach at porn shows anymore? What if Rachel determined that her methodology of sharing Jesus— which is an inherent part of her personality and therefore a gift from God—wasn't enough anymore and decided to join the crowd of protesters outside the porn show, yelling through a bullhorn that everyone inside was going to hell?

What if, instead of living in and embracing the small, Rachel decided to *manufacture* something big? What might have become of Brittni then?

Look, I'm not saying that big things aren't good or that we shouldn't be on the lookout for the extraordinary. I would even say that there are times and situations that call for something big and extraordinary.

But those times are few.

And we can't become so enamored with those times that we turn them into the be-all, end-all of our lives. If we try to live for the extraordinary, gigantic moments, we're putting our focus on the completely wrong things.

Instead we must learn to treasure the ordinary in our lives. The day-in, day-out interactions we have with those around us. We must put our emphasis on developing the right hearts—hearts that are completely submitted and surrendered to Jesus—and then keeping our hearts focused squarely on Him.

Because then Jesus can bring the extraordinary down into your ordinary.

## Chapter 3

# DEFINE EXTRAORDINARY

Let's talk about language for a minute. Not swearwords or anything like that—I mean the actual words we use every day. Let's take, as a case study, the very ordinary word *silly*.

When I tell my young daughter that she's being *silly*, what do I mean? Generally I would say something like that to her if she's goofing around and having fun and just being the little girl that she is.

If I were to tell my wife that she's being *silly*, what would I mean then? Besides inviting a whole lot of heated feedback from my wife, I might mean that, in whatever conversation we happen to be having, we have different opinions about what we think is important—and that hers is wrong.

But here's the crazy thing about the word *silly*: it took a very, very long road to develop either of those meanings, or any of the other ones we assign to it today. Did you know *silly* started off with a religious connotation? In the Middle Ages, which is around the time the word first surfaced, if you told someone they were *silly*, you were giving them a compliment by saying they were obviously blessed by God or very pious, which certainly adds a different spin to a phrase like "silly Christians," doesn't it?

Eventually some people focused more on the *goodness* aspect of *silly*—if you were a devout believer who was blessed by God, then you must be very good—and so *silly* began to take on a meaning that related to innocence. A *silly child* wouldn't be one who was hamming it up in the back of the car or singing into her hairbrush—it would be more like a thoughtful, wide-eyed child who embodied purity and unspoiled kid-ness.

But, as is usually the case with a word, years of using *silly* in this way eventually led to a blunting of that focus on innocence and goodness; some English speakers shaped the word into something more like *harmless*, like a passive child who didn't talk back at the dinner table. And from there, it was only a short step to start using *silly* to mean someone who should be pitied. That *silly child* just sits there and doesn't have any drive or ambition.

Once you start dumping negative connotations onto a word, it's tough to turn it around to mean something positive again, and that's exactly what happened with *silly*. By the 1500s, *silly* carried the weight of *weak* or *feeble*; and once you're using a word to call people weak in the body, it's easy to start applying that to their minds.

*Silly* was shaded the color of *foolishness*, which outside of being *knocked silly* is pretty much where we find it today, though with far fewer teeth. While people probably started using that *foolish* business with the intent of it being a real insult, *silly* has morphed into a harmless type of foolishness. From *blessed* to *foolish*, with a lot of stops in between. Language can be a silly thing.

The point is, we all have ways we define things, and those definitions can be colored by many different factors. Even today, a word like *chips* can mean two very different things, depending on whether you live in the United States where *chips* are crunchy things you snack on, or whether you live in the United Kingdom or Australia where *chips* are fried potato wedges that accompany fish or hamburgers. That's a geographic factor.

That same word, *chips*, can conjure up different images depending on your upbringing or income level. Just ask for descriptions of *chips* and you'll get different answers from a schoolchild (they'll probably offer up *potato chips*), a baker (*chocolate chips*, anyone?), or a gambling addict (*poker chips*).

And yet despite all these facets of linguistics, our culture seems to have an all-purpose definition for the word *extraordinary*. Or for the word *success*. Or, especially when it comes to doing things for Jesus, words like *big* or *important*. While those words can field a lot of different specifics, we tend to see them all in the same light.

But when it comes to something as monumental as the kingdom of God, those words are all painfully, woefully inadequate descriptors. They don't even come close. Not by a long shot. They're drops in the ocean of God's ideas of success and importance, of what Jesus would call big or extraordinary.

Because what looks big to us can be incredibly insignificant to Jesus. And what we think is nothing—a simple smile and a compliment, for example—can be the very thing Jesus uses to rescue someone from a seven-year life of making pornography.

We've gotten it all wrong.

Nothing is too small for Jesus.

Nothing can be so big and important that it impresses Him.

With Jesus *everything* is one size fits all. And that size is the size of His kingdom.

The sooner we learn this, the better—especially when it comes to the ways we do outreach.

Can I let you in on a dirty little secret from the world of organized religion and nonprofit ministries? This isn't usually said out loud in the church world—and many, if not most, church leaders may not even realize this is how they think—but it's subtly understood that numbers determine outreach "success." How many people "got saved" versus how much was spent to reach them. No one would really put it in this kind of terminology because it sounds cold-hearted, but it's true. Many churches and ministries look at people coming to Christ as a return on their investment. That's how they determine success.

Once you write it down, though, the ridiculousness of that type of thinking becomes universally clear—because

Jesus doesn't play by our rules or restrictions. I heard someone say on the radio recently that you should be able to
share Christ with anyone in under three minutes. Really?
This is how we're representing the gospel, as an elevator
pitch that you would use for your business or screenplay
idea? People who don't know Jesus are skeptical and want
to see how you're living this out, and they likely aren't
going to be convinced in a three-minute conversation—it
may take three hours, or three months, or three years.

Or seven years.

Let's go back to Brittni—the porn actress I mentioned
in the last chapter who came to know Jesus partially as a
result of XXXchurch's porn show outreaches—and Rachel,
the XXXchurch volunteer who built a relationship with
Brittni over the course of seven years. During those seven
years, Rachel had a chance to talk about a lot of ordinary
things with Brittni. She didn't try to hit her over the head
with Jesus or force some sort of commitment or prayer out
of her—they just chatted about life, about being women,
about stuff that, on the surface, feels pretty inconsequential
and small.

Yes, Rachel would bring up her faith as the Holy Spirit
gave her occasion, but the point of any conversation the
two of them had was never Rachel trying to get Brittni to
sign on some dotted line of Christianity. Rachel wasn't
trying to close a sale—she was trying to get to know
someone who was deeply lost and hurting, but who didn't
know that yet.

Let me tell you—I've talked to a lot of lost people, and many of them already know the basics of the gospel. There aren't many people—not in the Western world, anyway— who don't know who Jesus was, who don't know about sin and redemption and the story of the cross and the resurrection. It's an integral part of our culture.

No, what lost people want to know about is not some gigantic Jesus rally or whatever; they want to know how *you're* living. How you function as a Christian in the everyday world. They won't care about Christ if you're a jerk to them because of their beliefs or their occupation or their sexual orientation. Or if you only invite them to your church's Easter service but don't ask about their kids. Or if you won't have them over to your house for dinner because they might use a swearword in front of your dog.

They want to know if you're consistent. If what you *do* matches up with what you *say*. And those things you do? Those are the ordinary things that don't make it into the ministry newsletter or get thousands of retweets.

Brittni was drawn to Rachel's consistency in the midst of the mundane conversations. Because that consistency revealed something about Rachel's character—it revealed that she *cared*. The truth is, everyone who volunteers alongside XXXchurch.com can spend thousands of dollars to go to these porn shows to hand out Bibles and tell people that Jesus loves them, and it's usually a mind-blowing time of interacting with people who desperately need Jesus. The conversations we have and the seeds of the gospel we're able to plant are genuinely humbling and magnificent. It's impossible to go on one of those outreaches and not come away changed.

And yet one of the most deflating things that can happen is when we come home and begin sharing the stories of what Jesus did in our lives while we were at the porn show, only to have someone ask, "So how many people did you rescue out of porn?" or "How many people got saved?"

They want a number.

And the true answer—"I don't know!"—is not good enough for many of them. People want to know results *instantly.* They want the numbers and they want them now.

Which is the great thing about big, extraordinary events—you can get those numbers right away and trumpet them in social media and on your website and in a press release to all the major news organizations. You can feed the meter and show a return on your investment.

But is that what Jesus did?

Yes, Jesus spoke to some big crowds—huge ones that would get Him a lot of publicity and airtime today—but the people in those crowds didn't gather because He advertised some huge event. Jesus didn't buzz-market the Beatitudes or platform-release the Sermon on the Mount.

Jesus did incredible, miraculous things during the course of His ministry—which was only about three years of His life, I might add. He probably spent most of the time leading up to that doing ordinary stuff like studying and mystifying His parents, but if you look over the Gospels, you'll see that Jesus spent quite a bit of His time hanging out with His disciples.

Twelve people.

He went small. On purpose.

And what do you imagine Jesus talked about with His disciples? Those guys did a lot of walking around from town to town, so they obviously got into some discussions. I know when I go on road trips, while I can have some pretty heady conversations with my wife or friends, usually we wind up talking about random things. Stories from childhood or fun memories.

Ordinary stuff.

Can you imagine Jesus—during the all-important, history-changing course of His ministry—hanging out with His disciples and just cracking jokes? Or telling a funny story about growing up as the son of a carpenter? I doubt Jesus was a nonstop joke machine, but I also doubt He spent the majority of His time as the self-serious wisdom-spouter that we often imagine Him to be.

Jesus spent most of His time interacting with only twelve people, and though much of what He did wouldn't make the news, it changed the world.

---

XXXchurch has been fortunate enough to be around for twelve years now, meaning we've had the opportunity to build relationships and show what a long-haul life with Jesus looks like. As a result of our efforts, we've started to see more and more people come to know the redeeming love of Jesus. We've seen tons of ordinary people get help for leaving behind a life of pornography; we've seen countless marriages healed; and we've seen young men and women clean porn out of their lives after being inspired by something they read online or by seeing a friend using our accountability software on their smartphone. It's pretty cool how many "little" stories we get to hear along those lines.

But when it comes to the big, headline-grabbing stories of some porn star defecting from their occupation in order to become a pastor or nun—those stories are few and far between. The porn industry is still going strong—in some respects, stronger and more profitable than ever—which can become a little disheartening. It's very easy to look at the tidal wave of pornography and feel like anything we're doing as a ministry is just a drop in the bucket.

That mentality has affected some of the people who have done ministry with us, to be sure. I've had more than a handful of people who have ministered with us over the years become tired of getting what seem to be no results. They've decided their efforts were a waste of time or money and have gotten discouraged.

To that I've always tried to say, "Don't think that!" Why? Not just because I want to keep them around our ministry, but because it's simply not true! Our broader culture has convinced us that such a mind-set must be accurate, but it's a particularly insidious lie to think that your work or your life must be based on getting "tangible results." If you're doing what you feel Jesus is calling you to do, then regardless of any laughably measurable outcomes, you're operating as part of His kingdom.

You're making a difference, whether you know it or not.

When you smile at that stranger, you could be saving his or her life.

I recently gave a sermon on this topic, about how we Christians in the church tend to treat evangelism as a checklist. We encounter people throughout our days and, instead of being people with hopes and dreams, despair and failures, they become items on the list, and it's our job as Christians to make sure we place checkmarks next to their names in the "Did Witness To" box. If we have to put checkmarks in the "Did Not Witness To" box, then we've failed in our duty and, likely, are directly responsible for sending them to hell.

In my sermon I talked about how this mentality of sharing our faith can really mess us up, putting the emphasis on "closing the deal" rather than exhibiting a life that is being constantly redeemed and renewed by Christ. I talked about my long friendship with Ron Jeremy, who is the undisputed king of porn stars and is such a legend that people line up to meet him and shake his hand. I've gone all over the United States with Ron, and no matter what town we roll up to, he never fails to draw a crowd of enthusiastic fans.

I've been friends with Ron for years and, at the time of this writing, he's still wavering about needing a relationship with Jesus. We've talked and talked and talked about God, about Jesus, about heaven and hell, about life with Christ and life without Christ—if it has to do with faith, Ron and I have covered it. While we've become really good friends, and while Ron knows where I stand on everything, he's still not entirely convinced he needs to turn his life over to the Lord.

In this sermon I also related the story I wrote about in the previous chapters—about the former porn star Brittni, how we managed to minister to her over the course of seven years, what that looked like, how the Holy Spirit convicts people at different times and in different ways, and how Brittni's conversion was exactly what the Lord had in mind for her but may not be what He has in mind for others.

I talked about how these things happen on God's timetable, not mine. Not yours. Not the church's. I talked about how, in general, evangelism takes time and usually requires building some type of relationship with people first.

After I gave this very wonderful, very biblical sermon, the senior pastor got up, thanked me, and, as was standard routine in their church, gave an altar call—and no one came forward.

No big deal, right? Wasn't that the point of my entire message? That God will do His thing in His time?

Except to the people on the leadership team of this church, it *was* a big deal.

When that service was over and we all met backstage, this church's leaders and pastoral staff were *freaking out* with all sorts of questions. Why had there been no response? Why didn't anyone come forward at the end? Was it the song the band played—was it too heavy-handed? Or maybe it wasn't heavy-handed enough? Was it the language the pastor had used in his invitation—was it too grace-oriented or too works-oriented? Was it something else entirely that they couldn't put their finger on, like lighting or sound issues?

I wish I were making this up.

Like many evangelical churches in America today, this church had multiple services on a weekend, and this service had been the first one for that particular weekend. The church leaders immediately began planning what they could do differently for the remaining services, specifically to get a conversion or two at the conclusion of each one.

Why? Because whether they realize it or not, in their minds they have to have numbers. They have to produce.

In the end the leadership at this church decided to change the song the band would play at the end of the service and rearrange the order of some of the closing bits of procedure in order to get more people to come forward. It's as if we were on an episode of *Survivor* trying to light a fire for the first time: you just keep trying and trying until you get the thing done.

But do you see what's happening in their definition of *success*? Not only are they deciding that success equals a certain number of people coming forward during the altar call, but they're defining it with the wrong focus.

It's all on them.

The idea that the Holy Spirit might not have convicted anyone to come forward—or that He was, but people were actively resisting it—didn't occur to them. No, the burden of conversion rested solely upon their shoulders, with none of it on God's.

Shouldn't we all take a step back and say to God, "I don't think You necessarily *need* my song or my sermon or my story or my video to do what You want to do." Isn't that the uncomfortable truth behind God's sovereignty? That He uses us and gives us value and purpose, but that He doesn't *rely* on us in the same ways we rely on one another?

Would that church be any less valid if they didn't see a salvation that weekend? Would their ministry to their community be any less effective? Would their members suddenly begin backsliding into a pit of moral depravity?

Let's take it a step further: in the long run, could this air ball of an altar call actually have been a *good* thing for this church and its leadership?

Here's why I say that: I've been a part of something big and extraordinary, and one thing I've noticed about it is that when you see God using you in those types of big environments, it's very tempting for that to go to your head. The *thing* can very easily become bigger in your eyes than God is, and guess who's at the center of this very big *thing*. You are. Suddenly it has become all about you and not about Jesus.

That's a bad, bad definition of *extraordinary*.

And it will mess with your head.

Instead, let God be the One who defines your life. Not just words like *success* or *extraordinary*, but also words like *normal* and *ordinary* and *small* and even the word *life*.

*Chapter 4*

## WHO YOU WERE CREATED TO BE

My wife tells me I am not the most romantic. I'm not necessarily a giant fan of flowers; but I do appreciate the delicate beauty they bring to the world. Though I'm not going to learn how to grow roses in my backyard, for example, I will purchase flowers for my wife every time I am driving and have to cut over from the 101 freeway to the 134. There is a great shop there that has a bouquet of roses for $7.99. I always make that purchase.

When you think about it, flowers are some of the most ordinarily extraordinary things we have on the planet. They make the place look nicer and smell nicer, for one thing, but then there's all the scientific stuff we don't notice—the business with bees and pollination that helps keep mankind alive. You know; no big deal.

But while flowers in general are some of the best small things we have, there's one particular flower I want to focus on right now, one that botanists have given quite the mouthful of a name: *Selenicereus grandiflorus*. I'm not even attempting to provide a pronunciation key, because from here on out I'm just going to refer to it by a more common name, which, in the interest of full disclosure, it shares with a couple of other types of flowering plants: Queen of the Night.

This is a fascinating plant. A species of cactus originally found in South and Central America, the Queen of the Night exhibits very interesting behavior, especially for a flowering cactus. The Queen of the Night only blooms—at the most—one night per year.

For 364 days of the year, the Queen of the Night is just a plain old cactus, sitting there doing cactusy things like being green and having sharp spikes and being a special nuisance when the kids kick the soccer ball into the shrubbery by the front of the house.

But then comes the night—the one night—usually in late spring or early summer, when the Queen of the Night stops being ordinary and becomes extraordinary. On this one special evening, this unique cactus will put out any number of tremendous, white, royal-looking flowers, while no one is watching, usually fully blooming around three or four o'clock in the morning. By the time dawn arrives, the flowers are wilted and withdrawn, gone for another year.

We could look at this another way, saying that on this one night of the year, the Queen of the Night reveals itself for what it truly is. It shows its true nature.

It does what it was created to do.

The rest of the time it sits dormant, looking, in all

honesty, pretty darn plain. I mean, maybe you have a thing for cacti, but I'm not a big fan of the look. There's not much of what the majority of us would consider inherently attractive in a cactus—and yet, on that one special night, the Queen of the Night comes alive with delicate beauty and fragrance. This is the extraordinariness that was there all along, that we just couldn't see because it wasn't time yet.

My favorite thing about the Queen of the Night is that it doesn't bloom during the day. Ever. If you don't know what Queen of the Night is or looks like in its nonflowering state, you could have it around your house for *years* without ever knowing what it was doing in the secret, quiet stillness of that magical, special evening. Even if you happened to get up in the middle of the night for some reason—to go to the bathroom or to get a drink of water or to let the dog out— the odds are 1 in 365 (that's a 0.27 percent chance, by the way) that you'll get to see the Queen of the Night for what it is, for what God created it to be.

Those flowers don't bloom for us. They don't bloom for the people who keep the cacti in their yards. They don't even bloom for the wildlife that might happen to be around. They won't be added to anyone's garden or make their way into a bridal bouquet or into a centerpiece on the cover of *Martha Stewart Living* magazine.

Those flowers bloom because *that's what God had in mind for them.* Though no human would naturally see those flowers without making a substantial effort to notice them, God *does* see them, and He rejoices in their beauty.

The Queen of the Night doesn't get a whole lot of recognition from humans. But God sees it. And He loves it. In fact He delights in it.

The Queen of the Night does what it does for the glory of God, just as it was created to do. In this instance, it's all about knowing your role in creation.

---

One thing that always cracks me up when I talk to people and tell them about my history as the "porn pastor" is when they hear about the people I've met or the porn shows I've attended and they say, "Oh, I could never do what you do." It cracks me up because I inevitably think, *Good!*

Not that I want exclusive ministry rights as the porn pastor—I just know that's been my role, that's been the place God has given me in ministry, where He created me to be for the time being. It's something I've understood as being unique to me and the team at XXXchurch, but I've also understood that it's not something that's for everyone.

Everyone has a place in the kingdom of God, and that place is unique to each person. Your place is unique to you. Not everyone can be the senior pastor, or the worship leader, or the person who adjusts the faders in the sound booth to create the perfect audio mix, or a member of the construction crew who built the church building, or part of the team of architects who designed it, or the person who surveyed the land long ago, or . . . you get where I'm headed with this.

It all comes down to discovering who God created you to be, then growing into that role—regardless of how seemingly small it may look to the rest of us.

As long as we're talking about roles in the local church, let me tell you about an extraordinary individual my family has uncovered at CCV San Dimas, the church we attend in Southern California. Before we started going to this church, I already knew a few people who went there, so when we finally decided to make this our church home, we already had an idea of the lay of the land, of the vibe of this particular family of believers.

Yet on our first Sunday morning there, the first person we encountered as we walked in the doors from the parking lot was a stranger to us—and strange *looking* as well. He was a giant of a man: burly, outdoorsy, and sporting a huge, overflowing beard. Think of a younger Santa Claus who happened to be a park ranger instead of Father Christmas, and you'll have a pretty good picture of this guy.

And he was reaching out his hand to us, a big smile on his face.

Now, if you're even remotely familiar with the evangelical church in America, you probably already know what this guy was doing—he was what is known as a *greeter*, someone, usually a volunteer, who stands at the door, shakes people's hands as they walk in, and welcomes them to the service. It's a way of making sure parishioners see a friendly, familiar face as they come to the morning worship service. Most greeters are also able to provide helpful information to anyone who might be visiting for the first time.

I didn't think we needed any helpful information, and since my daily world is filled with a lot of meeting people, I tend to steer clear of church greeters when I'm going to church as a regular congregant instead of speaking at one. But this guy? This guy was different. He had it *down*. This bearded giant was a naturally outgoing guy who was imposing but approachable. Plus, since he was such a big dude, he was kind of difficult to avoid.

We walked in the doors and he shook my hand, my wife's hand, and the hands of my two kids. He asked our names and we gave them, and he welcomed us heartily to church that morning. No big deal. We went in, participated in the service like everyone else, and that was pretty much that.

Except on the way out, after the service was over, we saw this same guy, in the same spot, telling everyone good-bye and wishing them a good day. Oh, and he was *using everyone's name*. Ours included.

The guy was sharp. Best greeter ever.

We try to go to church as regularly as we can, but my schedule involves a lot of travel to speak at different churches across the country and sometimes in other countries, so we aren't necessarily there every Sunday. I know a lot of people have their routines, their specific services they attend and the special pews or chairs they always sit in. When I was growing up, my parents had "their seats," and everyone knew to stay out of those seats.

My family is not like that. We go when we are able, which makes it especially handy that this church has multiple services on a weekend. Sometimes we go on Saturday evening, sometimes we go to the early service on Sunday morning—okay, that doesn't happen very often—and sometimes we go to the later service (don't tell anyone, but sometimes we don't go at all).

The point is: my family's church schedule varies quite a bit. But no matter which service we go to, we see this guy. He is *always* there, always greeting people, always with the big, genuine smile and the friendly handshake, always knowing everyone's name and using it.

The guy's a legend, so much so that my wife, Jeanette, and I sometimes talk about him when we're not at church. We try to imagine his origin story (remember chapter 1?): where he came from and how he became the best church greeter in America. Like I said, church greeters are usually volunteers, but this guy has the chops and skills to be a pro. Jeanette actually began to suspect the church pays him—he is just that good.

We also started to wonder: Does this guy do this for *every* service *every* week, or is it just a coincidence that he's there whenever we are?

I got the definitive answer one weekend when our church had me preach the sermon for every service. This is a busy church that has two services on Saturday evening, as well as three on Sunday morning, and a final weekend service on Sunday night.

Six services.

Guess who was at the door for each one of them.

Yes, I spoke six times that weekend, but while I was in the greenroom before and after each service—sitting on a couch, eating my little snacks and drinking water from a little plastic bottle—the Santa Claus of greeters was out there shaking hands, smiling, engaging people, memorizing their names, and making the most of every tiny interaction he had with every person who walked in or out of those doors.

And you know what? He loves it!

It's very easy to walk by this guy every week and think, *Oh, he's just the greeter,* but that's not true, any more than the worship leader is "just a singer" or the senior pastor is "just a person who talks about the Bible."

No, this man—standing out there every service of every weekend—is a living, breathing example of a person knowing his role and owning it. This church greeter is doing *exactly* what he was created to do, and he knows that about himself, accepts that about himself, and lives it every time those church doors are open.

I got so intrigued by this greeter that I finally approached him one Sunday, asked his name (it's Ken), and told him about this book and how I was using him as an example. I asked him how he got started in the greeting game, and his answer surprised me.

"Someone showed me love when I didn't deserve it," he said, "and that was the model I wanted to pass on to other people. Everyone needs to be shown that acceptance."

Greatest ever.

In fact, in our conversation he referenced Matthew 10:42, where Jesus talks about small things—like handing out cups of cold water to little kids—reaping big rewards. This is exactly what Ken does, and he knows it.

"I take great joy in shaking hands," he said. "I volunteer because I love the Lord, and I get blessed more than anyone when I see the joy in people's faces. This makes my week."

I asked him how he felt about being a greeter instead of something more "important" like a pastor. His answer floored me and was actually a perfect summation of this book:

"Being a pastor would be a step down."

As humans in a Western culture, one of the questions we tend to ask as we look around at our dissatisfied world is the big one: "Is this all there is to life?"

So now my question to you is this: What if the answer to that question is a resounding, "Yes! Isn't it great?!"?

What if the so-called *small* thing of shaking hands and smiling at people at the church door is your highest calling? What if you're meant to bloom once a year, at night, for a purpose that is apparent only to God?

There can't be very many of us—if we answer honestly— who, when we dreamed about what we were going to be when we grew up, sat around and thought, *I want to be the best church greeter around.*

I don't even think this guy did that.

But there he is. Maybe he uses those skills in his day job, which makes it easy for him to translate them to the front door of the church. Or maybe he *doesn't* get to use those skills, making it all the more fun for him to be able to serve God with them on the weekends.

Maybe, while the rest of us tend to want the "bigger" job, this guy has seen a job that few people classify as big, and by doing it with such huge amounts of joy, he is turning it into the biggest job he could possibly have.

Don't get me wrong—I'm not saying we shoot for the lowest common denominator or give up on our dreams. We shouldn't lower the bar or forget about the big stuff. We should always be striving to give God every ounce of ourselves in pursuit of His kingdom. The crazy fact I learned about Ken when we met up was that he is actually an ordained minister but is serving in the exact role that he believes God has called him to.

What I *am* saying, though, is that we all have our roles for bringing that kingdom about, and we need to let God define that role for each of us. Only then can we operate fully in our roles. For a very few of us, that role is being onstage and preaching; for another select few that role is standing at the door and shaking hands. The rest of us have our roles somewhere in between—and for some of us that role may have nothing to do with the church at all.

If God's called you to be a church greeter, don't lower yourself to become a pastor.

If God has created you to be the Queen of the Night, why would you stoop to being a rose?

Many church missions focus—or used to focus, anyway—on something often referred to as the 10/40 Window. If you've been around the evangelical church in the last twenty-five years or so, you've probably heard this term more than once—maybe even thrown it around yourself—without even really knowing what it means or what it stands for.

For the record the 10/40 Window refers to latitude, the section of the globe between 10 degrees and 40 degrees north of the equator. This encompasses most of northern Africa, all of the Middle East, and pretty much all of Asia, making it an area of the world that contains almost two-thirds of the total population, much of which has little exposure to Christianity. This, of course, makes it the perfect target for Christian evangelism efforts, and many sincere and wonderful mission efforts have focused on reaching the massive population in this part of the world.

Many missionaries have been called to the 10/40 Window and are doing great work there. It's exotic and otherworldly and makes for a compelling newsletter; and it's easy—and tempting—for the rest of us stuck in our home countries to look at this and think one of two things:

*I wish I could be doing something big for God's kingdom like these people do!*

or

*I could never do something big for God's kingdom like these people do!*

Hopefully you're starting to get the point by now, but my question to you is this: Instead of the 10/40 Window, what if you're called to the Nine-to-Five Window? What if your missions opportunity is lying at your doorstep, at the office, at the stores you frequent, or in your own home?

What if we need to rethink the notion of doing something big for God's kingdom?

What if we're attaching the label of *big* to something that He finds unimportant or unimpressive? What if the ordinary, small things of life are what you're called to?

How would you live your life then? Would you wither away in quiet desperation, always looking for the next big thing, or would you step fully into whatever role God has called you to?

We don't encounter these much anymore—at least not in most modern evangelical churches—but surely you've seen a stained-glass window. Back before we had modern electric lighting, churches needed tons of windows. Eventually, during the Middle Ages, priests and church leaders in charge of teaching the truth of the gospel to a bunch of people who couldn't read (on a historical scale, widespread literacy is a *very* recent phenomenon) hired craftsmen to make stained-glass windows that portrayed images from the Bible, like the Old Testament Bible stories or key scenes in the life of Christ. That way they could teach something about the character of God to parishioners who couldn't read it for themselves.

These window artisans would take shards of colored glass and, through careful selection and arrangement, create breathtaking art from them. Every piece of glass served a purpose in the context of the artwork. Whether it was a seemingly important part of the image—like a certain shade of blue glass used as the eye of Jesus—or a seemingly ordinary part—like a different shade of blue to make part of the sky surrounding a crucified Savior—*every piece had its place.*

You can't have the completed masterpiece without every piece being exactly where it needs to be.

Now think of the kingdom of God; think of what God is up to in the world today, in your life and in the lives of those around you. Think of that as a stained-glass window, and think of yourself as one of those shards of glass He is using to make His masterpiece. He knows where you need to go. He has just the spot for you. You just need to trust Him as the artist and let Him put you there.

Of course, there's also the opposite danger—of letting people elevate you beyond positions that God wants you to have. It doesn't happen often, mind you, but it does happen, especially in this celebrity-rich culture, where far too many of us crave fame.

When I think about this, I recall a couple of times in the New Testament where we see this dynamic at work. First there's a story about Jesus we can read in the Gospel of John, chapter 6. Most of us know the story of Jesus miraculously feeding the five thousand, which is in itself a very cool story of a man knowing exactly who He was and what He was about. Of course, that man was Jesus, so . . . you know. But in the Gospel of John, we can also read about the fallout from that miracle, some ramifications that don't get talked about a whole lot on Sunday mornings.

Something to keep in mind about this story is that it took place in the midst of the Roman Empire. The thing about empires is that they don't just happen. The Romans didn't build an empire by going to a country and asking nicely if they could rule. No, the Romans created their empire by force, building it on a foundation of violence, bloodshed, and oppression. If you lived in a place that had not been conquered and you happened to look up and see a Roman army on the horizon, you knew you were in trouble. Plain and simple, they were going to come into your country and take it over. The end. Thanks for playing.

Here Jesus was, in occupied territory, exhibiting some pretty miraculous power. Now imagine you were a citizen of a country that was conquered by the Romans and you're pretty tired of having these outsiders ruling over you and telling you what to do—and probably taking most of your resources for their own ends. But what could you do? You weren't strong enough to resist the might of the Roman army.

But this guy? This miracle-working guy? Yeah, *He* probably could.

After Jesus did His food-multiplying miracle—in front of thousands of people—those same people probably began to think Jesus could liberate them from Roman oppression. He could be the guy to finally overthrow the current Roman government and become the new king of Israel. This could be exactly who they'd been waiting for!

And that's what the people tried to do with Jesus. They started talking among themselves about prophecies and kings, and began formulating plans about making Jesus their new ruler.

But Jesus wouldn't have it. No, He was all about His role. He knew what God wanted Him to do, and nothing was going to deter Him from that—so we find out in John that Jesus took off by Himself to a mountain in order to avoid the rabid mob intent on installing Him as king.

There's another story along these lines, though this time it comes from the book of Acts and involves the apostle Paul, a guy named Barnabas, and a bunch of pagans in a town called Lystra. Paul and Barnabas were on a missionary journey, preaching about Jesus and the gospel and following whatever directions the Holy Spirit gave them.

As they preached, Paul noticed a guy sitting down who had a birth defect that had prevented him from ever being able to walk. As Paul talked, he noticed this guy and how intently he was hanging on to every word Paul said. Paul could tell this man was receptive to the gospel and to the power of God working in his life. So Paul paused his sermon, looked at this dude, and said, basically, "Hey, man. Stand up."

Huh? Okay.

The guy leapt to his feet and started walking around.

And the crowd went nuts. They knew this man, knew he was physically incapable of standing, but they also saw with their own eyes that he was now walking around. Miraculous!

As proof that missing the point completely is not merely a modern affliction of Internet comment threads, this crowd of people completely missed that Paul was giving glory to Jesus through this healing. It was through the power of God—and not just any god, but the *one true* God, Jehovah—that this man was now walking. Paul hadn't done the healing; God had.

Yeah, the crowd didn't catch that part. Or maybe they just didn't *want* to catch that part. Regardless, they jumped to the conclusion that Paul and Barnabas were gods who had come to them in human form—specifically, the people thought Barnabas was Zeus and Paul was Hermes, who, among many things, was a messenger for the gods in addition to being a god himself.

There was a big commotion, and a priest from the temple of Zeus started bringing in livestock to sacrifice to Paul and Barnabas in order to appease them. Paul and Barnabas weren't having it, though—they went into the crowd and showed them that they were just humans, like everyone else, and pointed the glory right back at Jesus.

Paul and Barnabas could've gone along with it for their own gain or to get access to the powerful leaders of that place. Remember the way the rebels tricked the Ewoks in *Return of the Jedi* by convincing them that C-3PO was a deity? Like that. But that wouldn't have been following the Lord or accepting their role in the story God was telling in that city.

The people of Lystra wanted to elevate Paul and Barnabas and make them a big deal, but it was up to Paul and Barnabas to check that and to say, "No, we're not a big deal! We're ordinary, just like you are! *Jesus* is the big deal you're looking for."

They had to own who they were and all that entailed.

They had to be who God created them to be.

We all do. God created us to be big on His terms, not ours.

Who are you? What's your big deal?

Own it.

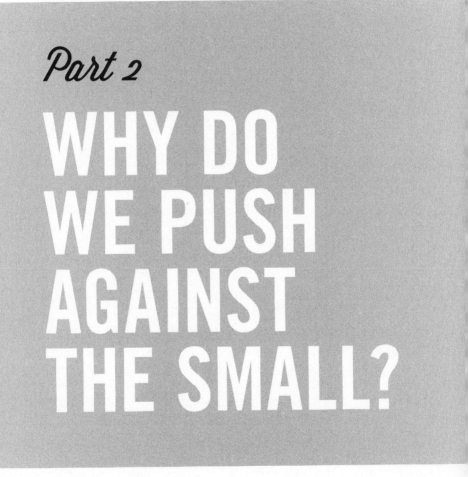

*Part 2*

# WHY DO WE PUSH AGAINST THE SMALL?

## Chapter 5

# WHO MAKES THE RULES?

If you know anything about me, you know I'm not too crazy about rules. Well, maybe that's not entirely true—I mean, I drive only a little above the speed limit and always accept the terms and conditions when I update my iTunes software. I guess it's better to say that I'm not crazy about rules that make no sense, or prohibitions that exist solely for the sake of the prohibition or to make someone in power feel more powerful.

Some rules in our culture are unspoken—they're the things you have to figure out on your own or learn through observation as a kid. If you're playing pickup basketball, you have to learn to call fouls on yourself or eventually you'll alienate all the other players and have no one to dunk over. If the valet loads your luggage for you, you need to slip him a few bucks as a thank-you for his trouble, whether you asked him to load that luggage or not.

These are the types of rules—or we might call them social norms—that we accept without thinking. It's just the way it is, and it's the way it's always been, and it's the way it will be for the conceivable future, on and on until the end of eternity.

But then there are other sorts of rules that we swallow without consideration. Rules that tell us we have to believe certain things about ourselves or about someone else. Societal assumptions we make about a person based on the way they dress or what they're wearing on their head or how much they weigh or what gender they are or how light or dark their complexion might be. These assumptions might be so ingrained in us, so subtle, that we do not even realize we're making them.

Storytellers love to play with these assumptions. How many movies, television shows, or commercials have you seen where the hotshot motorcyclist or racecar driver removes the helmet only to have a bunch of luxurious hair come spilling out of it? Turns out that all along the driver was a *girl*!

Today it's easy to look at stories about the civil rights movement in America in the 1960s and have our minds blown at how anyone could have ever thought about race in such a backward way. Why? Because our rules and assumptions are different now than they were then. Though, I must say, we aren't even *close* to being finished with the hard work of rooting out racism in its entirety.

Even though I say I'm not a fan of rules, I am grateful for them. Without rules, without conventions, without social assumptions, we'd likely have anarchy on our hands. We would not know how to talk to one another or how to find a place of agreement on many issues. When you think about it, language itself is a series of agreements—we've all agreed, at some point in the past, that this language is English and that each of these words means a specific thing—that's how you're able to comprehend the message I'm delivering by using these specific words.

Why? Because rules indicate by their mere existence that someone has discovered the "right" way of doing something. That someone has gone ahead of us in the jungles of life and existence and forged a pathway to follow. Those are the rules. That's how we tend to think about them.

Have you ever traveled to a foreign country and learned the hard way about the unspoken rules of behavior or communication there? My friend Adam, who is listed on the cover of this book as the coauthor, once lived in the African nation of Uganda and learned, over time, that much of their communication is rooted in gestures and facial expressions instead of actual words. Yes, here in the United States of America we have nonverbal communication, but that's more of an understood type of communication—a series of facial tics and postures and hand cues that either embellish what we're saying with our mouths or give an indication of our mental or emotional state. Here nonverbal communication is usually an enhancement, an add-on.

In Uganda that isn't the case. Adam told me he was completely adrift when it came to the subtle and understood forms of communication there. No one informed him that, for example, when you raise your eyebrows, you are saying, "Yes," and, occasionally, agreeing to whatever the other person is talking to you about. This could be problematic when haggling over the price of a head of cabbage in the market and, as an American, you raise your eyebrows in disbelief over the outrageous asking price. Whoops. You just bought it.

No one told Adam that, should he feel the need to wave to the street children (these are often orphans or children from the village whose parents send them into town to beg for money for the family), he should wave with his palm completely open, pivoting at the wrist. As Americans, we're accustomed to waving to children with our hands extended, fingers together, then bending our fingers up and down, pivoting at the first knuckle like we're scooping out sand for a sand castle at the beach. It's tough to describe in print, but you know what I mean. It's how we wave to kids here.

In Uganda if you wave to kids like that, you're telling them to come to you; and if someone tells a street kid to come to them, it's most likely because they're going to give them money or food. The innocent American might wonder why they're suddenly surrounded by these bright-eyed, expectant children, not knowing that the kids were just doing what they'd been asked to do. Because those are the rules over there. It's just what you do.

In addition to rules, there are formulas. We *love* our formulas. Don't believe me? Just go to the self-help section of any bookstore and flip through a few of the bestsellers.

You'll find formulas left and right. Seven ways to get out of debt; three easy keys to a perfect marriage; fourteen surefire principles for social media success for your business. They're everywhere. The Internet is especially built on formulas.

Netflix—the media company that started out as a subscription service that sent rental DVDs in the mail and has since become a major player in content streamed over the Web—understands this. Since so much of its content—namely, movies and television shows—is viewed online, Netflix is able to keep track of many different metrics.

When you stream something on Netflix, the company computers record what you watch, what devices you're using, how often you pause, whether you watch the whole thing, what you watch next, and many, many other pieces of data. They pay attention and break it all down into excruciating detail to get a good idea of each subscriber's likes and dislikes, looking for patterns in order to maximize that data for their company's profit.

Eventually Netflix tired of being a place where people could watch other companies' stuff and decided the time was right to start producing their own content as well. And when it came time to decide what they should make, Netflix executives turned to all those numbers they'd been storing and examined what their subscribers liked to watch.

Around this same time, an independent production company called Media Rights Capital had bought the rights to a little-known BBC series—a political thriller from the 1990s called *House of Cards*. They started developing an

American version of the show with director David Fincher and looked at casting actor Kevin Spacey in the lead role. They then started pitching it to many different television networks known for taking programming risks, including HBO and Showtime.

Netflix heard about this possible pitch and, since they were in the market for original programming, went to the numbers. They checked their data and found out that their users liked the BBC original show (which was already available for streaming on Netflix), liked movies by David Fincher, and liked movies starring Kevin Spacey. Their data told them this series would be a win, so they struck a deal with Media Rights Capital and bought the show.

They simply followed the formula.

While TV networks have ratings and film studios have box office reports, Netflix doesn't use any of those traditional tracking systems to gauge whether their programming is considered a success or a failure. Instead they have an internal metric that determines whether they've met their goals with a specific show. After *House of Cards* debuted, Netflix announced that the series was their most-watched TV title at the time. The show became such a phenomenon that it was subsequently honored at the Emmy Awards that year, the first time a show had ever garnered such acclaim without being broadcast on television. In fact this January Netflix won its first ever Golden Globe for best actress in this series.

We love our formulas even when they don't actually exist. Netflix's success with their formula aside, a common complaint among Hollywood screenwriters is that movie studios impose all sorts of formulas on screenplays in an effort to build success into the film. After the script has been tinkered with enough to ensure maximum acceptability among audiences, the production itself is often overseen with an eye toward formula in performances, art direction, cinematography, and other departments. Generally the idea is that, if some previous film made a dump truck full of money, then producers should just do what *that* film did. Then they can hand their address to the money dump truck delivery service, because they'll be needing it.

Makes sense, right? Except it doesn't work. Because while movie producers can have a general idea of what leads to audience satisfaction—happy endings tend to get better word of mouth than sad ones, for example—they simply cannot make an audience come to their film. No one can manufacture a hit; we're reminded of that every time a studio pours buckets of cash into a big summer movie only to see it wander through the box office like a tumbleweed in a Western.

Someone once observed that there is no formula for guaranteed success, though we'd like there to be. We know this because, if there were a formula, there would be no such thing as a flop. Every film, every television show, every music album, every book or magazine or other piece of commercial pop art would soar into the Piles-of-Cash Hall of Fame.

And getting back to rules, here's another little quirky thing: as I've been talking about pop art being *successful,*

I've been speaking pretty much on terms of it succeeding commercially. That is, I've been equating success with dollars—and I didn't have to tell you that.

Why? Because that's another one of the rules of our culture.

You're making money? Then you're successful.

It's how we've built our society, like it or not. Those who have dollars are considered successful; those who don't, aren't. And so we chase down formulas and patterns and rules and predictability to see if we can figure out how to be *successful*.

It's easy to fall prey to this thinking, even in the church world. Recall my story from a previous chapter, about the church that tried tweaking their formula at the end of the service to compel more people to come forward during the altar call. I'm not talking about liturgy as formula—that's different. I'm talking about churches creating or searching for a predictable formula in order to get results—often leaving out the possibility that the Holy Spirit is going to be the One to get those so-called results.

And again I ask: Who writes the rules?

Who uncovers the formulas?

And why are we so eager to listen to these people? Why do we so casually swallow or endorse or live with these rules and formulas?

When God created the world, He created it to have certain patterns, which is probably where we get our love of predictability. We know the sun will rise in the morning and set in the evening. We know it's going to get relatively cold in the winter and relatively warm in the summer, though where we live will dictate how hot and cold. As a current resident of Southern California and a former resident of Michigan, I can speak to this from personal experience.

We know that seeds are for planting, and then, after a little while, crops are for harvesting.

Rhythms. Patterns. Seasons. Those are predictable to a certain degree. Those are, in a sense, formulas.

But sometimes days are cloudy and we never see the sun. Sometimes we get mild winters or freakishly spring-like summers. Sometimes seeds are planted but drought or infertile soil or never-ending thunderstorms ruin the harvest.

We can expect the seasons, we can anticipate the patterns, but we're still going to check the weather apps we have on our phones to see how we need to dress for the day.

The odd thing is, while we love predictability and formulas, we don't see them very often—if at all—in the Bible. Think of the times we read about Jesus healing someone by taking a specific action—whether it's healing the man who had been born blind by making mud out of dirt and saliva and plastering it on his eyes, or when He healed the woman with the issue of blood simply by letting her touch His cloak, or when He raised a little girl from the dead by holding her hand and speaking two words to her.

Every time a person had an encounter with Jesus, He did something different. Unique. We don't have any Gospel accounts of Jesus raising anyone else from the dead in the same way. After some time He yelled at the dead Lazarus, who had already been entombed by the time Jesus got there. We don't see anyone else with a long-standing illness jostling to get a piece of Jesus' hem, though the Roman centurions did argue over the fate of His clothing while Jesus was being crucified. We don't read about Jesus or the disciples marketing and selling a special Blindness Removal Mud to help support their ministry and spread brand awareness.

No, Jesus treated every opportunity, whether it was seemingly a big deal or not, individually. The only formula He applied was, "What does this person need, and how will it bring about the kingdom of God when I give it to them?"

Here's an interesting side note. In the gospels of Matthew and Mark, we do see Jesus feeding two giant crowds of people—once when He fed the five thousand with five loaves of bread and two fish, and another time when He fed four thousand with seven loaves of bread and an unspecified number of fish. In both instances He had the disciples break everyone into groups, and in both instances He blessed the food through prayer before breaking it up and distributing it.

Does this count as a formula? I don't think it does. I would file this more under Jesus providing a consistent demonstration of God the Father's sovereignty in wanting to meet the needs of the people. Everyone in the crowd was hungry—not everyone in the crowd was blind, or chronically ill, or dead.

The moment we start looking for formulas or rules is the moment we start thinking *we're* in charge. Do we begin to believe that if we say *this* prayer in *this* way or perform our church service in *this* order or do *this* thing or *that* thing that God will honor our efforts with His blessing? That He's kind of on the hook to do what we expect?

Are we trying to force God to obey *our* rules? To fit into *our* formulas?

Do we think we know better what God needs for His kingdom than He does?

Do we sometimes think too much about ourselves—put the focus on our own desires, our own happiness, our own thoughts and goals and dreams—instead of letting God inhabit those things for us, in us, and through us?

Are we uncomfortable with letting God do what He wants, even if that flies in the face of our formulas, rules, and expectations?

He's the One who makes the rules. And those rules pretty much are: He gets to do what He wants to do, and He wants you to join in on the fun—whatever that looks like.

## Chapter 6

## UNDER PRESSURE

I'm going to give you two names: Workhorse and PAC. These are not the names bestowed by parents upon young, innocent, helpless children. They are pseudonyms for a pair of street artists who work primarily in New York City.

If you're unfamiliar with the term *street artists*, they are probably what you're thinking—painters who use buildings or other public spaces instead of canvases to create their works. If this is new to you, the chances are pretty good you heard the term *street artist* and immediately thought of graffiti, so let me set the record straight here. Yes, while most street art is technically graffiti, not all graffiti is street art. This isn't petty vandalism or marking of territory— street art is the work of dedicated, serious artists who, for the most part, are interested in showing society something it hasn't seen before, usually to make people think or to make a cultural statement. For example, you may be familiar with an English fellow who goes by the name Banksy, who is unquestionably the world's most famous street artist.

Anyway, most major cities worldwide are teeming with artists like this, who revel in the thrill of turning something ordinary into something unique using only a cardboard stencil and a can of spray paint. Not only are they creating art but they're also doing it illegally and tweaking the establishment. Incidentally, for a fascinating and humorous look at this world and the circus that now surrounds it, I recommend watching the documentary *Exit Through the Gift Shop*.

Since modern street artists are making art in a time when just about anything can be bought or sold, this type of artwork has become commercialized. An artist can create street art that is meant to be bought by collectors and installed in their homes or studios. A cottage industry has grown around this phenomenon, and now street artists are finding a little money in what they do. Some of Banksy's artworks have sold at auction for hundreds of thousands of dollars, for example.

Which brings us back to Workhorse and PAC, two guys who are not opposed to selling their art, but who also worry the commercialization of it will have a negative effect on their work.

When you live in one of the largest cities in the world, it's tough to find a little alone time; so PAC took to hanging out with a friend who participated in a pastime known as urban exploration—which is basically just walking around and looking into the hidden corners of a city to see what can be found. In due time PAC and his explorer friend came upon an abandoned subway platform somewhere underneath

New York City—they refuse to say where, exactly. PAC knew it was love at first flashlight-illuminated sight.

PAC began visiting the platform on his own time and exploring it with powerful lanterns, soon discovering that it led to other platforms that collectively covered the area of a football field. At some point in the past, the city had begun constructing these platforms; when plans changed and the new platforms were abandoned, they were left with no electricity, no staircases or escalators in or out, and no tracks for the subway trains. Basically they were just big, open, underground spaces with a lot of flat, blank walls.

You or I, should we happen upon that platform, would see a dark, dank space that we would want to get away from.

PAC saw an art gallery.

He began to spend more and more time at this platform, just hanging out and enjoying the solitude of knowing the city that never sleeps bustled relentlessly above him. He soon met Workhorse, who specializes in creating street art in abandoned spaces, and couldn't resist showing him the subway platform. While they were down there, an idea that had been brewing within the two came to fruition; they called it the Underbelly Project.

The Underbelly Project became the modern, street-art implementation of the ethic "art for art's sake." Workhorse and PAC put the word out to their closest street-art friends, extending invitations for them to come to this newly christened underground gallery and create a work of art that would never be seen by anyone but the artists themselves.

Little by little, the Underbelly Project took shape as artists from across the world scheduled some time in New York City to contribute their creative voices to the unique exhibition. It wasn't easy, though. Getting to the platform gallery space required the crack timing of a jewelry heist and not a small amount of patience and agility. The artists had to linger on an active platform until it was no longer occupied, jump down on some tracks, and walk to the abandoned platform—and they had to do it without being seen by law enforcement or anyone working for the city, since they could get arrested for trespassing.

Because of this thrilling and semidangerous route to the gallery, once they were down there the artists weren't able to leave the platform to get any materials they might need mid-creation, so they had to bring in everything at once. Paints, stencils, and in one case a table, two chairs, and a formal dining set—all of it was brought in by the artists on their one and only scheduled time to create.

The platform was humid, adding another layer of complexity for the artists to overcome. Those who specialized in working with paint found that their compositions would never dry, so some began to incorporate this into their artwork. PAC, for example, put the constant dripping to his own purposes in his piece. Rather than become frustrated with the space's refusal to compromise for their artistic visions, the Underbelly Project artists rolled with the punches to honor the quality and context of the space they were working in.

Eighteen months after it began, the Underbelly Project was completed. Workhorse and PAC, hoping to contribute to the artistic community and to spark conversation, allowed a reporter from the *New York Times* and another reporter from the *Sunday Times Magazine of London* to tour the gallery, take a few pictures, and write about it, so long as they didn't reveal the location of the platform-turned-gallery nor the real names of anyone who worked on it.

After that, they left.

They haven't been back since.

The reason this story is so unique—the thing that makes it news and worth discussing in this book—is the fact that these artists were quite literally underground. They *didn't want to be famous* for this art show. They weren't out to make themselves into a big deal or to turn the art world upside down.

They just wanted to do it, with no cultural pressure, with no one to impress, with no desire to showcase anything to the world.

Just because.

In today's world, *that* is pretty darn unique.

---

Cultural pressure is such that the big thing—the outlandish thing, the flamboyant thing, the creative thing, the biggest, brightest, noisiest, craziest, most vulgar, most explosive, most outrageous, most divisive thing—seems to get all the media attention. Sure, you can eat sixty-eight hot dogs in ten minutes, but no one will talk about you because Joey Chestnut, a professional competitive eater, can eat sixty-nine of them—at least at the time of this writing. Competitive eating records tend to fall rather quickly, so for all I know someone else has broken the plateau of seventy hot dogs in ten minutes, which is the competitive eating equivalent of the four-minute mile, I guess.

If it isn't big, it doesn't lead the evening news. It doesn't get 3,000 shares and 10,000 Likes on Facebook. It doesn't get retweeted 85,685 times (or favorited 57,682 times) on Twitter, like whenever Justin Bieber tweets something bland. (Note: those are actual numbers as of this writing for a Bieber tweet saying, "Great night.")

Social media is filled with people who are outraged about something and who cry out, "We need to make this go viral!" But you can't *make* something go viral, especially if it's greeted with a collective shrug by the world at large. What's big to you may not be big to everyone, especially if it doesn't have enough superheroes in it.

The story of the Underbelly Project is newsworthy precisely because it cuts against the grain of what we expect from artists in the modern times. These artists did all this hard work just to let their stuff rot away in some abandoned subway platform that no one can visit. No one will see it. More importantly—no one will *buy* it. If these artists can't sell it, if they can't convert it into Instagram followers or see it reblogged on Tumblr, then why would they even do it in the first place? What's the point?

And let's face it—we feel this way ourselves sometimes. If you say something on Facebook that gets a lot of Likes, it's validating, isn't it? It makes you feel as if what you had to say was important. That, in the cultural economy of social media, means you *matter*.

While I was forming the outline of this book, I hopped on Instagram and saw a photo of a friend of mine. She took this photo in her closet, in front of her mirror—her phone is clearly visible in the photo—and her head is turned sideways to showcase that she has put her hair in a ponytail. Her caption for the photo was: "It's a ponytail kind of day." The photo got twenty-seven Likes from her fewer than three hundred Instagram followers.

Look, I'm not saying it's wrong to have an Instagram account—I have one: find me at CraigGross—or that it's wrong to post a selfie of your ponytail, or even that it's wrong to Like a selfie of someone's ponytail. None of this stuff is wrong.

I just want to point out that it *exists*.

And then I want to ask a question: Why?

Why do we do this stuff?

What kind of response are we seeking when we post these types of photos?

What's going through our minds as we flick through our Instagram feed, see this type of photo, and tap the heart to Like it?

Why, why, why?

Is this the way we're trying to turn the ordinary into the

extraordinary, the small into the big? By posting it? By liking it? By commenting on it? By littering it with emoji?

It's fascinating to see the ways that something like social media, specifically Facebook, has completely transformed some of our cultural conventions. Social media gives us importance—it gives a personal, unique space on the Internet where we can be who we want to be, trumpet the political opinions or religious convictions we want to shout out, promote ourselves or our products, or just crack jokes.

When Twitter first hit the scene, some funny and enterprising people immediately saw the potential to expand their audience, and they came out swinging. Twitter is, indeed, a practically perfect joke-delivery mechanism, with the ability to share humorous thoughts among diverse networks of people. Some of these self-made comics gained a significant following and parlayed those numbers into careers as stand-up comics or writers for television or film. Several Twitter users have even turned their popular and witty observations into best-selling books.

But it isn't just entertainment—we also use social media to keep ourselves informed. When news breaks, the world turns to social media for updates, and people on the scene rush to be the first to report some new twist in the story—even if it means they don't get the facts straight. Who cares about getting the story right if you can be the *first* one to get the story *mostly* right and generate some buzz about yourself? Maybe you can even start trending!

Likewise, who cares if social media amplifies our inherent

loneliness or creates the illusion of community with our online "friends," while subtly separating us from our physical, real-world families? I'm getting Likes over here!

Again: I'm not against social media—I'm an early adopter and love to use it to share small portions of my ministry or life with the world. But I do see how many of us are mistaking this very ordinary thing for something extraordinary, and I just want to encourage you to keep your priorities in proper order. Social media, while it can be a helpful tool, is really pretty hollow on the whole.

Can I tell you from experience how false the world of social media is? Let's talk about the unquestioned champion of the worldwide social media landscape: Facebook. Facebook is the place where Likes have become a kind of currency—the more Likes your page can get, the higher profile it can have in the Facebook algorithms and the more weight you can carry in the artificial kingdom that is Facebook. But none of it matters. And I can prove it.

There's a shoe company called Creative Recreation that my son, Nolan, and I both happen to love. They make the coolest shoes in low tops and high tops, and I'm not gonna lie, I have quite a few pairs of them. They're fairly affordable, and the company is doing some flashy stuff with something as simple as sneakers. Nolan and I are both pretty infatuated with them.

Right before Christmas last year, Creative Recreation had this photo contest on their Facebook page. To participate, you took a photo of yourself doing whatever you like to do in your Creative Recs, then uploaded that photo to their Facebook page. Each day all the photos were judged according to the number of Likes they got, and the winner would get a hundred bucks, plus the chance to face off at the end of a month against all the other daily winners to determine an overall contest winner. The top two finishers in the overall contest would win $2,500.

Well, that much money sure would buy *a lot* more pairs of shoes, wouldn't it?

I thought it would be cool to enter this contest by doing a father-son photo of myself and Nolan, so we started brainstorming and figured out a cool idea. Nolan is an actor, and since he's a growing kid who is constantly in the process of looking different, he had to get some new head shots—professional photographs that are sent out to agents and casting directors so they can see what an actor looks like. We were headed to a photo shoot, so I threw all our pairs of Creative Recs into a duffel bag and took them to the studio. After the shoot, I dumped all the shoes out on the floor and sat down with Nolan in front of a white wall for our photo. It was nothing special, but it was a cool father-son moment—the two of us bonding over our love of a specific type of shoe.

I entered the photo in the contest, then tweeted and blogged about it and got enough of my followers to click over to Creative Recreation's Facebook page and vote for us to win the daily contest. Hello, one hundred dollars. Plus, now we had that sweet invitation to the big dance.

When the month was up and all the daily winners were

decided, the new contest page went live. It listed all the photos, again on Creative Recreation's Facebook page, where people could vote for their favorite photos by liking them. Once that page went live, I shared the link with all my social networks—Facebook friends, Twitter and Instagram followers, Tumblr subscribers. If I had a Pinterest or Google+ account, I would've blasted it on there too. I wanted the money, sure, but I'm really competitive anyway, so I also wanted to win something from our favorite shoe company.

After about a day, I'd pretty much exhausted all my social networks, and everyone who was going to go like our photo had already done so. I didn't have anyone else in my circles to help us out. But we started out in the lead and, after a couple of days, had about three hundred Likes—which was a lot more than the next-highest vote total. If the voting wound up being based solely on picture coolness, I was sure we had this thing in the bag. I mean, there were a few good photos among our competition, but most of them were just okay, and ours was the best by far—at least it was in my opinion.

But you see, this wasn't about the photo itself. This was about Likes. Why? Because if you tell all your friends to go to Creative Recreation's Facebook page and like your photo, that activity will show up on each friend's Facebook news feed, which will mean it shows up on all *their* friends' feeds, which will generate more and more exponential exposure for Creative Recreation's Facebook page and, by extension, the Creative Recreation brand. As a marketing strategy, it's pretty brilliant.

At this point the photo itself doesn't really matter—what *does* matter is how many people you can involve in the game; in other words how many Likes you can generate. You don't need to have a good picture; you just need to have Facebook accounts who like your photo. And what do you know? This one guy who is also in the contest starts *blowing up* with Likes. His photo starts to bury everyone else's with Like totals.

This really puzzled me, so I did some digging and realized you didn't have to register for anything to vote in the contest, and you didn't need anything other than a Facebook account. There was nothing at stake in voting—all you had to do was click Like.

Well, guess what's for sale? Facebook Likes.

And they're pretty cheap, actually. If you do some digging, you can buy a thousand Likes on Facebook for about $25. Well, once I learned this, it was *on*. Maybe this wasn't my proudest moment in life, but since the contest wasn't technically about having the best photo but about having the most Likes, I did some more Internet research and, after weighing all the options, took the plunge.

I bought some Likes.

The contest boiled down to our photo and this other guy's photo; and it turned into a real horse race, actually, going back and forth and back and forth. First we'd have more Likes; then he'd have more; then we'd get some more and then he'd miraculously add a whole bunch more to his total. After I made contact with a guy in India who sold me all my Likes, he really got into it and worked hard to make sure our photo won. We wound up beating the other guy by 40 Likes with only a half-hour to spare. It was thrilling—as thrilling as a social media contest can get, I suppose.

Anyway, we won.

When I told Nolan, he was a little confused and started to wonder if the way we'd won could be considered cheating. My take at the time was that, while it was a photo contest *in spirit*, it was a Like contest *in actuality*, so buying Likes was simply outsmarting the competition. The other contestants hadn't been wily enough to think of that, and we'd found a way to come out on top.

After having some time to think about it and reflect, I'm not so sure. I'm starting to wonder if I didn't buy into our cultural notions that having more Likes is the same thing as having more happiness. Because, if I'm going to be honest, I have to admit there is a side of me that would enjoy having more Likes. Why? Because that *feels* better. It *felt* great to win that contest, especially because I was able to beat that other guy at his own game.

But in the end, what did I gain? Some money and a stark reminder that sometimes I care way too much about stupid stuff on Facebook.

Once I step outside the insanity of competition, I can see how this is all just wind in the trees anyway. Facebook Likes, Twitter followers, Instagram followers—they're all for sale. While I was working on this chapter, I got a spam e-mail from a company offering a buy-one-get-one sale on YouTube views—buy a million views and they'll throw in an extra million views at no cost. You can inflate your social media ego all you want for just a little money. You can get one thousand Instagram Likes in a few minutes, and it only costs you five bucks. I know this for a fact because I did it, to see if it really worked. So, about those people you look up to because they have more friends than you or more followers, just think: if Jesus was on Twitter he might never be verified and would be fine with only a few followers. In case you don't believe me about buying Likes, followers, and views, check out www .fiverr.com and see what you can get for five bucks.

And this is where we're turning, as a culture, to find our validation. To find our importance.

But it isn't real.

It isn't art—it's just graffiti on a very public wall.

Now that I've spent the entirety of this chapter talking about how fake the social media world is, I suppose it would be nice to end the chapter with a reminder of how much genuine good can come from it.

Sometimes good springs from a tragedy, which is the case of a little girl in the Pacific Northwest whose name was Rachel Beckwith. Rachel's family attends a church in the Seattle area called Eastlake Church, where they heard about a nonprofit organization called Charity: Water that works to provide clean drinking water to developing nations around the world.

Rachel heard about Charity: Water and decided she wanted to do her part to help those around the world who did not have access to something as fundamental as clean water. Rachel's ninth birthday was rapidly approaching, so instead of birthday gifts, Rachel asked that people donate to her Charity: Water account. Her hope was to raise $300.

Her birthday came and went, and while she did indeed receive quite a few contributions, she fell a little short of her goal. No matter, though; she had done something truly wonderful—albeit small—by giving of herself in order to help others. How many nine-year-old kids would find happiness in going without birthday presents, anyway?

Tragically, however, Rachel Beckwith's ninth birthday would be the last birthday she would ever have. A few weeks after turning nine years old, Rachel was involved in a horrific traffic accident when a semitrailer struck a logging truck, causing a chain reaction that sent enormous logs onto the highway and the semi into the rear end of the vehicle that was carrying young Rachel.

She was critically injured and died three days later.

Somehow the word got out about Rachel's now-expired birthday wish, to raise $300 for clean water for kids in other parts of the world. Someone decided to honor Rachel's memory by making a donation in her name to her birthday account, which was still active.

Then someone else. Then someone else.

Word began to spread like wildfire across the landscape of social media, and the contributions poured in. The more the story spread, the more donations accrued to Rachel's account, and soon the story of her final birthday desires—and the social media world's sudden interest in it—was picked up by national news outlets like the *New York Times*, CNN, and NBC News, among others.

Then her story went international. More and more people from around the world began donating to Charity: Water in her name, until the final tally for her account was in the vicinity of $1.2 million.

From less than $300 to $1.2 million. That is an astounding example of goodness being harnessed by social media after people's hearts were touched by a truly tragic story.

A year after Rachel's untimely death, her mother, Samantha Paul, traveled to Ethiopia to visit some of the many communities benefiting from clean water as a direct result of Rachel's birthday wish. In a story for NBC News, Ms. Paul was quoted as saying, "The biggest thing I'm looking forward to is seeing the actual wells where the people, because of Rachel, are going to be able to have clean water, seeing other 9-year-old children and their moms knowing that they're going to have a 10th, 11th, and 12th birthday and so on because of Rachel's heart."

On the whole Rachel Beckwith's goal was pretty small. But it came from a big heart contained within a little girl.

There is nothing that is so small that God can't turn it into something big.

## Chapter 7

## "LOOK AT ME!"

We hear a good pop song and think, *I could write that.*

We see a piece of art by someone like Jackson Pollock or Georgia O'Keefe and think, *I could paint that.*

We go to the movies to watch a buddy comedy and think, *I'm just as funny as either of those guys. I could be in that.*

We watch our favorite sport—which just happens to be the sport we played when we were in high school—and think, *If only I had really pursued it, I could be playing that.*

You get the idea.

Many of us feel that we inherently have something to share with the world at large. I would say that even introverts or the melancholy can feel this way, though those feelings can get self-focused and warped into the opposite type of reaction, when we can think, *No one cares about me.*

But we wouldn't have thoughts like those if we didn't *want* someone to care about us, to take an interest in what we believe or feel or think. To hear our opinions and validate them.

Regardless of who we are, we are looking for acceptance. Some of us are looking for it on a stage in front of thousands, while others of us look for it on a metaphorical stage that is in front of our spouse, or our parents, or our siblings, or that girl or boy in math class that we really have a crush on.

We think, *If only something were different, then I could be doing that.*

We could be doing something big. And *then* we'd be important.

---

My buddy Jefferson Bethke is a poet. He's actually an amazing poet. You ever heard the term *wordsmith*? That's Jeff. He can take words and punctuation and hammer them into something that goes far beyond a collection of letters and sentences—something that, combined with his unique recitation, reaches into your soul and speaks to you in a deep, connective way.

Jeff and some of his friends made a video of Jeff performing his poem "Why I Hate Religion, But Love Jesus" and posted it to YouTube, then shared it among their various social networks. And the thing blew up—before long that video had twenty million real views (not paid) and Jeff was the toast of the social media world. Interview requests poured in, as well as speaking and writing opportunities that kept him busy for a year. He even got a book deal out of it.

If you have something you want to share with the world, you can now do it very easily, but you can't force everyone to notice your stuff. You can only put it out there, talk about it yourself, and hope you strike a nerve so the rest of the world starts talking about it too.

But that brings up the question: Why do we want people to see our stuff? I mean, I'm no stranger to this myself—I am, after all, a person who has a high-profile ministry that thrives on media recognition. We started with nothing more than an idea and a means to generate buzz. I'm all for making noise online and in the media in order to attract attention to what you're doing—especially if what you're doing is all about the kingdom of God.

We all have a desire to be noticed. Even those of us who might want to blend into the background, who shun social media and crowds. We're all, in some sense, like little kids who crave their parents' attention at the oddest, most random times.

You know what I'm talking about—especially if you're a parent. At the beach, just before your child runs into the water, they turn around and shout back to you, "Hey, Mom! Hey, Dad! Look at me!"

"Look at me, Mom!" as your son tears around the playground, running up the ladder and zooming down the slide.

"Look at me, Dad!" as your daughter parades around the living room in a frilly ballet outfit, her toes poking out of a hole in her tights.

"Look at me!" as they jump out of trees, cram their mouths full of blueberries, or try to figure out (unsuccessfully) how the dog leash works.

It's all the same stuff we wanted to share with our own parents when we were kids ourselves—to make sure they noticed these random, ordinary, small moments of our lives. Maybe by noticing those moments, moms and dads fill them with significance for their kids. Maybe, in those times, the ordinary, mundane walk or jump or climb or funny face transcends ordinariness and becomes something special.

Something worth paying attention to.

Isn't it possible that this desire to be seen—this collective cultural shout of "look at me!"—is behind the explosion of reality television programming?

Yes, reality TV has increased exponentially partially because it is much less expensive to produce than its counterpart, known in the industry as scripted television. The fairly recent boom in niche cable networks—like Food Network, or HGTV, or the Travel Channel, or any of the other thousands of networks offering a specific theme of broadcasting—means many hours of programming to fill. And you can only show so many reruns of *Everybody Loves Raymond*.

So the networks—both broadcast and cable—have turned to reality programming to fill airtime. But they can't produce reality TV without two things: people to participate in whatever the camera gets pointed at and other people to watch those people on television.

And we won't run out of either of those two things anytime soon. Maybe never.

Reality TV is everywhere, from the seemingly unending

melodramatic spins of the "Real Housewives of _____"
variety, to competition shows searching for the next big
singer or entertainer or model or designer or culinary arti-
san or soccer star or bass player for a new rock supergroup
(I made up that last one, I hope).

There is, it seems, a bottomless pool of families willing
to allow access to their lives and have them plastered on
television screens across the world. Gone are the days when
people used to think, *My office could be a sitcom—there's
some crazy stuff that happens there!* Now it's more along the
lines of, *My office could be a reality show—and I could be
the star!* As I write this, a certain network is talking to us
thinking that our crazy ministry and characters around us
would be great for TV.

To celebrate their fiftieth year in broadcasting and to
increase awareness of their annual pledge drive, Thirteen,
the flagship Public Broadcasting Service station in New
York City created a subversive set of posters that they plastered across the subway system. These posters advertised
plausible (but ridiculous) reality TV shows with titles such
as *Married to a Mime*—the tagline was, *"She's* got plenty to
say!"—*Bayou Eskimos*, and *Knitting Wars*—"It's sew on."

The catch was that all the shows were fake. Parodies of
the reality TV shows we're all used to watching. The posters
looked authentic, right down to the smirk and crossed-arms
look the participants of reality shows give the camera in their
publicity photos—but they were all inventions of the advertising company behind the fund-raising campaign. The ads

pointed out that these shows were ridiculous yet plausible, demonstrating a sad state of affairs in the current television landscape. So shouldn't you support more thoughtful programming in the form of your local PBS station?

The ads were a hit. It was just the type of thing the reactionary—and, admittedly, smug—Internet culture would jump on and laud. It makes a great point: Maybe this reality television fad has gone on a little too long. Maybe not everything needs to be turned into a circus to be watched. Maybe ordinary stuff should stay ordinary. Maybe not everyone is cut out to be a celebrity. Maybe we should, as a culture, reconsider our priorities on celebrityhood anyway.

We are obsessed with celebrity, to the point where people become famous simply for being famous, for having famous parents, for having a lot of kids, for saying something outlandish on the radio, for doing something sexually suggestive at the Video Music Awards on MTV, or—you get the idea.

And it's easy to make fun of these things from a lofty position, but the fact is, they wouldn't exist if people weren't interested in them. Celebrity worship happens because *people want to worship celebrities.* They become fascinated by the ordinary parts of a celebrity's life, simply because those ordinary and small things are being done by Someone Famous.

But why do we treasure *those* ordinary things over our own?

Why do we look to outside sources for approval?

Who is the audience we're hoping for? To whom are we yelling, "Look at me!"?

If it's anyone other than God, the question must be asked: Why are we seeking approval from that person, or through that source?

It's one thing to want to be acknowledged by your parents, or your kids, or your spouse, or your accountability partner—these are people whom you have invited into your world, who are an irrevocable part of who you are, where you've been, and where you're going. You want them to look at *you* as much as you want to look at *them*—you are an indelible part of each other.

From there the circle of looking should grow a little larger until it includes people who are a secondary part of your world—your extended family, your next-door neighbors, your coworkers, people you wave to at church, the barista you're on a first-name basis with. Their opinions about you should matter to a certain degree, but shouldn't be the standard for your self-worth. If you're getting wrapped up in what your kids' friends' parents think about you—if you start desiring to have them notice you—then you're getting off track.

And then we have the rest of your social circle. I'd include your social media acquaintances here, and anyone else you see irregularly—like your weird uncle who lives in a camper in the desert, or the people at church you don't wave to, or the fill-in barista who comes in every now and then from a different store because she's trying to pick up more hours.

After that is everyone else—the people you don't know.

The *world*, as it were. And ironically, these are the people we seem to seek the most validation from—the theoretical audience for our personal reality television show, should some network finally see the genius behind it and put our lives on the air. If we could just get *them* to look at us, then we'd be okay. We'd feel accepted.

We wouldn't feel so ordinary.

We wouldn't be so small.

Best of all, if we could get to that point, then even the so-called *ordinary* things we do would become extraordinary.

If we went out to buy a pack of gum, photographers and celebrity news show cameras would inundate us.

If we went out to buy a pack of gum without first engaging in all our personal grooming habits in the morning, then we'd be on the front page or the lead story on the syndicated entertainment show.

Of course I'm being over-the-top with this, and in a lot of ways this sounds more like a nightmare than a dream life. But be honest: Aren't there aspects of this type of lifestyle that ring true to you?

If we could just make a name for ourselves, then we could finally do what we *want* to do, without worrying about money.

If we could just get our brand out there, we could land some clients and help some people.

If we could just get noticed, we could work out some endorsement deals and get even *more* noticed. And get paid for it along the way!

If we could just get more YouTube views, more Facebook Likes, more Twitter favorites, more activity on our Pinterest board, more Instagram comments, then—

If, if, if . . .

All in an effort to put the focus on us. To feel a little less ordinary.

You want to know something? You don't have to chase recognition in order to feel validated or extraordinary.

This may sound cliché, and it just might make you roll your eyes, but whatever your reaction, you can't make this simple statement any less true: Jesus notices you.

And He likes what He sees.

Honestly. That is the straight-up truth.

## Chapter 8

# THE ACCEPTANCE DISCONNECT

I asked some questions in the last chapter about why we seek validation and acceptance from outside sources rather than from God, and those questions sprang from my own sense of curiosity about where I land on the spectrum of acceptance. I mean, I'm pretty well known as a guy who can bring attention to what I'm doing, whether it's handing out our notorious "Jesus Loves Porn Stars" Bibles at a porn convention or driving around the West Coast in a hearse wrapped up in a giant, eye-catching graphic that reads "Porn Kills Marriages."

I like to get stares, especially if it brings awareness to our ministry—and, by association, the gospel. I know this about myself and am comfortable with it. It's part of my personality—which is a gift from God—to be an agitator, to be an iconoclast, to stand outside the norms and point at them and say, "You might want to rethink what you're doing here."

Which is why it may seem odd to now be in the middle

of a book that celebrates the ordinary, that encourages you to think of your life as much more than a highlight reel that skips over the boring parts that the rest of us call *everyday living*. But the great thing about my life is, while I get to do some pretty outlandish things in the name of Jesus, those things are not what define me as a person. If I have a *great* career as the porn pastor but am a jerk to my wife and am never around to parent my kids, then what kind of *greatness* have I accomplished?

I was once taping a piece about my unorthodox friendship with renowned porn legend Ron Jeremy for ABC's program *Nightline*, and a friend of mine happened to be there on the set with me. I had a lot on my plate for that day that made me seem really important—I had to do this interview for television, I had some ministry stuff to do, and I also had to take my son to his soccer game.

This friend of mine knew what I had on the day's roster; and as we sat in the midst of this television crew setting up and putting a spotlight on the place where I was going to sit for the interview, my friend turned to me, gestured toward all the crew and camera gear, and said, "You know all this stuff is BS, right? The only thing that matters on your schedule today is Nolan's soccer game."

And he was right! I could do all the interviews I want and our ministry could grow to never-before-imagined heights, but if I ignore the small stuff—the ordinary stuff— then I'm slacking on what's actually important: my family.

We all know this. Heck, it's the basic plot of just about

every heartwarming family movie from time immemorial—
that Mom and Dad are too caught up in whatever they think
is important and are missing what's *really* important the
whole time. This is nothing new.

And so we're quick to acknowledge it when it comes
to family—especially if we're parents. We understand that
our kids are important, and that sometimes we have to put
everything else in our lives on hold to tend to their needs—
also understanding they need to learn they are not the
center of the world, and that sometimes they'll need a little
patience with Mom's or Dad's schedule.

But back to us. Are we quick to accept the importance
of our everyday lives? Of reveling in the ordinariness of our
existence? Can we possibly believe that God smiles on us
even when we aren't doing something for Him? That He
thinks small things like sleeping or cooking or mowing the
lawn are really cool?

That He accepts us, no matter what?

That your life has value *just because you're you*?

It doesn't matter what the rest of the world says about
you—whether you know them or not, whether they're in
your workplace or at church or in your family. There is
only One whose opinion counts, and His opinion is that
He loves you.

You are accepted.

You are loved.

You don't have to chase acceptance from anyone else—
and that's good, because people are always, always, *always*

going to let you down. You can count on it. If you know someone, they are going to disappoint you in many ways, multiple times in your life—and you'll do the same thing to them. That is a plain fact and there is no getting around it.

This is the part of the gospel that we tend to get so wrong, when we believe we have to *do* something to earn God's acceptance, to stay in His good graces. That yeah, He accepted us when we were lowly sinners, but now that we've come to know Jesus as our Lord, we have to get our act together or we'll upset God and *really* have to work hard to . . . what? Get back on His good side? Make Him like us again?

Do we think Jesus only loved us when we were sinners because we didn't know any better, but now that we've been saved, we're on the hook? We have to hold up some end of the bargain?

Jesus will *never stop loving you.*

Jesus will *always accept you.*

Does He care about the way you live your life? Absolutely.

Does the way you live your life have any impact on His acceptance of you? Absolutely not.

He accepts the mundane, the low, the banal, the dreary, the monotonous, the humdrum, and any other word that shows up when you search the thesaurus for synonyms of *ordinary.*

You could live a perfectly quiet life—keeping your head down, doing a menial job with no chance for promotion, paying your bills on time, and smiling at people you encounter on the street—and be welcomed by God with open arms at the end of it, with Him embracing you with a hearty clap on the back and a booming, "Well done!"

God doesn't give a rip about what the rest of us call *acceptance*. He's calling the shots, and His perspective rarely looks anything like ours.

You know, one of the things that really keeps us going at XXXchurch is that we're not the most famous charity or ministry in the world. Because of what we do, many people—especially church people—hesitate to talk about us. Porn has gone mainstream since we started XXXchurch, but in many ways it's still a "dirty little secret," particularly among Christians.

Because our organization deals in shattering taboos and talking about the elephant in the room, we aren't necessarily considered the coolest or safest ministry to support. We're in this weird space of being too outspoken for a lot of mainstream churches, but too Christian for the mainstream media's full approval. I can write a blog for CNN or the *Huffington Post*, but they'll always file it under their Religion header and offer a disclaimer that says all the opinions are my own and not necessarily the opinions of the staff or editors of their site.

We don't have rock stars and celebrities showing up to our fund-raising galas. We are supported by a lot of musicians, but mostly ones who play music for fringe audiences—in other words, we're not expecting Justin Timberlake or Kanye West to step onstage in one of our "Jesus Loves Porn Stars" tank tops.

We think that's sort of awesome.

Would we like to get that kind of exposure? Of course we would—we're all about spreading the word about the dirty little secret of pornography addiction to as many people as will listen.

But we don't do this to get exposure. We don't do what we do so people will look at us and tell us how great we are. We aren't living for the continuously fading approval of the media.

We do it because this is what God wants us to do.

We do it for the marriage saved as a result of a husband or wife confessing their addiction and seeking help.

We do it for the kids whose parents have fallen into the trap of porn—parents who now see what they need to do to make their kids aware of porn, and to protect them from falling into the same trap.

We do it for the performers who find themselves trapped in a world they often can't get out of, despite their deep desire to do so.

We do it for Jesus.

When we're doing the bland, ordinary stuff of organizing trips or loading boxes of Bibles into a van or changing the oil on the "Porn Kills" hearse, we're participating in building the kingdom of God.

We're playing by His rules, not ours.

And He's turning those small things into extraordinary encounters.

You know what's actually a funny story when you think about it? The story of Adam, when God first shows him the garden of Eden.

Stay with me here.

In Genesis 2, we read the story of the creation, when God calls everything into existence and makes the entire world. And then God plants a garden in a place called Eden, an ideal land full of perfection and grace and natural wonder. It's everything a person could need—lush greenery to keep it shaded, a diverse collection of fruitful trees for food, and four different rivers that provide ample clean water for drinking and bathing.

When we think of the word *paradise*, the picture that leaps into our minds is probably something falling remarkably short of the garden of Eden. This place is heaven on earth—a glorious spectacle of nature that has all the great stuff about the outdoors (pretty scenery, delicious food, refreshing water) and, presumably, none of the bad (predatory animals, rough weather, mosquitoes).

Amid this grand natural beauty, this perfect paradise, God plunks down Adam—the first man, the pinnacle of all creation—into the garden. Then what does He say?

God tells Adam to take care of it.

Isn't that hilarious?

Have you ever stopped to consider what that even *means*? I would imagine that most of us don't pause there, because the very next sentence focuses upon the singular action that Adam *isn't* supposed to take—the part where

God tells Adam he can eat from any tree in the garden *except* the Tree of Knowledge of Good and Evil. It is very typical of us to look out for the rules to follow, to try to find what we're *not* supposed to do so we can make sure we *don't* do it.

But I want to back up and look at the command God gave Adam, what He specifically said to *do*. Because that is absolutely a riot if you look at it closely. It's the cutest li'l commandment in the Bible.

Again: God told Adam to take care of the garden. What do you suppose that would look like in reality? Was he supposed to mow the lawn? Trim the hedges? Spray pesticide on the fruit trees to keep the bugs off? Sprinkle some Miracle-Gro on the tomato plants to make them nice and juicy?

See what I mean? It's laughable! Because God gave Adam the easiest job in the world—to *take care* of a garden that was the utmost paradise. The thing could run itself without Adam's help. Adam couldn't make the trees grow tastier fruit or make the rivers run clearer or more efficiently. He couldn't make the animals get along with each other or implement a growth strategy for regional, national, and then global success.

Nope. I believe the way God meant for Adam to care for the garden was simply to use it. To enjoy it. To romp and play and just do nothing. Eden was created to be a playground for Adam to enjoy God's creation and then, once a day, hang out with God. It was a place where Adam could do pretty much whatever he wanted—except worry about right and wrong. He didn't even know about them yet!

It was an extraordinary place to do a bunch of really ordinary stuff.

It's the very picture of God's acceptance, of His love, of His grace.

And check this out: all the agricultural tricks to having higher-yield crops—you know, working the ground, planting seeds and reaping harvests, tending crops, and all that—all that *work*, was the first curse God laid on Adam after the fall.

In case I lost you, let me back up. In the creation story, after God put Adam in the garden, He then made Eve and put her in the garden with Adam. Then the two of them hung out for a bit, just having the time of their lives in God's playground. Then the devil showed up in the form of a serpent and tricked Eve into eating fruit from the Tree of Knowledge of Good and Evil, which she handed over to Adam so he could partake as well. Their disobedience got them booted out of the garden and into the wilderness we now call the real world.

Once they were kicked out, God cursed all three of them. The devil was cursed to eat dust, and God threw a messianic prophecy on top of him for good measure. Eve, on the other hand, was cursed to have pain in childbirth— sorry, women of the world.

And Adam? He was cursed to have to *work*. To sweat and toil in the dirt and grime in order to make a living.

Think about that for a minute.

Is it possible that our desires to *do something big* for God come from the notion that we can improve on the garden of Eden? When we get into work mode and start hoping to achieve big things for Jesus, are we actually reaching back for a time when Adam was cursed for his disobedience?

Are we uncomfortable just playing in the garden to the delight of the Lord?

Don't get me wrong, I believe in hard work—that's part of how things get done in this world. It's a fact of life and society, and it won't change soon.

I'm just wondering if maybe we need to get back to an Eden-guided viewpoint on work, placing less emphasis on the *doing* part and instead getting back to the God-breathed, God-ordained life of *being*.

That's grace.

That's the gospel.

As long as we're talking about planting and gardening and all that, and because we have other stories in the Bible that use garden imagery in the context of the Jesus part of the gospel, let's move this conversation in another direction. I'm thinking specifically of a letter the apostle Paul wrote to the church in Corinth.

In 1 Corinthians 3 we read about some church members who were in a major argument about who they should be following. This was a church Paul had obviously visited, preaching the gospel and helping the church and its members get started in the rhythms of gathering and worshiping together. At some point after Paul's stopover, another guy named Apollos had come through and done some ministry in this church, and it seems that some people had come to Christ while Apollos was there.

This church was in a big disagreement about who they "followed." The people to whom Paul had originally preached were all, "We're followers of Paul!" while the people who came to the church while Apollos was there said, "Forget you guys—we're followers of Apollos!" It must've been enough of a problem that Paul had to address it in his letter to the Corinthians, which he does by saying, "Look, you guys, we're just planting seeds and watering here—it's God who makes things grow."

I'm paraphrasing, by the way.

Now I'm going to step away from the paraphrase and drop some of the actual letter on you. Because after saying that, Paul wrote: "The one who plants and the one who waters have one purpose, and they will each be rewarded according to their own labor. For we are co-workers in God's service; you are God's field, God's building" (1 Corinthians 3:8–9).

In other words—we're just doing our thing, whatever God has called us to do in His kingdom, and we're going to let God be the one to reward us.

And in modern times it's easy and tempting to hear this and nod our heads along with what we're hearing and think, *Yeah, exactly.*

And then go back to *working hard.*

So we can *get results.*

For whom?

And who are we kidding here?

Do we have a problem doing the ordinary things, like planting seeds as Paul did, or watering as Apollos did, because we want to see the fruits of our labors? Is it tough for us to be okay with doing the simple work of watering when it often means we will have to move on to something else, away from the thing we watered, before there's any budding, any blooming, any fruit to be harvested?

Are we uncomfortable with planting or watering through ordinary interactions because that means we may not see how it all turns out in the end?

Have you ever had a garden? How long does it take to harvest fruits and vegetables from a garden, compared to the length of time it takes to actually grow those fruits and vegetables? You can pick a tomato in a couple of seconds—a tomato that you carefully cultivated over a few months.

I'm wondering how many of us exclusively want to be harvesters—and my guess is most. I'm also curious as to whether we only consider harvesting to be the major work of the kingdom of God, the reward, the thing that we're here on this earth to do.

I'm thinking we should take a few steps back to look at this process the same way God does—that it's a long haul requiring a lot of planting and watering. Which, in the grand scheme of things, is really easy, especially when you consider the transformation a seed undergoes to turn into a fruit-bearing plant.

You know what most of gardening is? It is waiting.

It's doing a bunch of other stuff while God does His thing in the ground. It's coming by every now and then and splashing water on the plant, and that's about it. Sure, there are things you can do to give your plant a better chance of taking root and thriving. For example, you can pull weeds from a bed, or you can plant your seeds in rich and fertile soil, or you can use pesticides to keep bugs away; but those are more maintenance tasks that assist the plant—they aren't necessary for growth.

Planting and watering.

And a whole, whole lot of boring, ordinary waiting.

You know: God stuff.

*Part 3*

# HOW TO
# GO SMALL

## Chapter 9

# GET SLOW

On her blog Ann Voskamp has an introductory letter that contains five very profound words: "Life is not an emergency."

Think about that statement for a moment. Let it sink in. Now ask yourself: How often do I treat life as if it *is* an emergency? How often do I rush around trying to get from one place to the other? When I'm driving, how many times do I switch lanes in order to get around the next car, and then the *next* car, and then the one after that—all so I can beat that yellow light before it turns red? How many times have I rushed through the grocery store or the coffee shop or the wherever-I-go because I had to *be somewhere*?

What would happen if you didn't have to be there?

What would happen if you scheduled some slow time into your day?

Would the world stop spinning?

Would everything collapse?

Or would you just . . . finally . . . breathe?

Note: this would be a good place for you to stop and take a deep breath.

Remember Adam, my friend who used to be a missionary in East Africa? This is a place that has running water, workable roads, decent infrastructure, mobile phones, wireless Internet—and absolutely no sense of time. If you go to East Africa with the intent of imposing your Western way of scheduled life on it, you will only get more and more frustrated.

Adam told me that within a week of living there, he'd tossed his wristwatch in a drawer. When it came time to leave and come back to the United States, he gave it to one of his African friends, a young man who understood the concept of *mzungu*—Western, scheduled-down-to-the-minute—time.

The battery was dead by then. The young man didn't care.

He probably wasn't going to use it anyway.

The obsession with time is definitely a Western thing, and especially an American thing. We are really, really into schedules and planners and calendars and synching our appointments to all our devices and making sure we're punctual, even though we hardly ever are.

Since I do a lot of traveling, I fly all the time; and it cracks me up how departure and arrival times are always given to an exact minute. You're telling me that this flight is going to leave at *exactly* 5:48 p.m. and arrive at *exactly* 10:58 p.m.? How do you know those times down to the minute? Because I've never had a flight leave *or* arrive at the exact minute listed on my boarding pass.

This doesn't exist in many other cultures. Adam told me that he had to learn how to deal with the laid-back, time-ignoring culture of East Africa. If he tried to live an American lifestyle there, he knew he would eventually go nuts with frustration; so instead of stacking his day full of appointments and chores, he would have *one goal* to try to accomplish that day. It could be something major like helping to plant the garden, or it could be something minor like going into town to pay the water bill. Either way, if he got it done that day, it was a successful day.

He didn't always get it done. Paying the water bill was especially tough. That place was *never* open.

Adam also said you had to learn that the phrase "come back tomorrow" didn't mean there what it means in the United States. If you go to a store here and they're out of something, and an employee tells you to "come back tomorrow," you know they're going to be getting a new shipment of whatever they're out of and will have plenty of them back in stock the next day. You may even ask what time their delivery truck comes, and then what time they think the merchandise will be available for purchase—so you can fit it into your schedule, of course.

The same does not hold true in East Africa. If you go to a store and they are out of something, they will tell you to "come back tomorrow." But that doesn't mean anything is on order. They are not expecting a shipment or a delivery, and there is no set time for any packages to arrive. It just means, "We don't have it now, and I don't know when we'll get it, but we may have it tomorrow, so you can come back then and find out."

You could be told to "come back tomorrow" day after day after day and *still* not get what you were hoping for. Because that's just the way things operate there.

We Americans would look at a system like that and find it maddening, flat-out dumb, or even—dare we think it—irresponsible. *How can you expect to keep customers with such shoddy service? You'll go out of business!*

Another aspect of African culture Adam had to get used to was the way the locals thought about time itself. Remember that watch? Here's why it was no good: if I tell you to meet me somewhere at 3:00, you're going to figure out how long it takes you to get there, plan ahead for traffic, subtract that from 3:00, and then leave your house early enough to get there *by 3:00*, right? Because in our culture it's rude to keep someone waiting. In fact, if you want to make a good impression, you'll even try to be a little early.

In East Africa if you make plans for an African to meet you at 3:00, they would likely not be there at 3:00. Why? Because 3:00 is likely when they would leave their current location to start their journey toward you. If they show up by 3:57, they are not considered late—because they have still arrived during the three o'clock hour.

And if they happen to meet someone along the way that they know, whether it be a family member or an old school acquaintance or their brother's friend's sister, they might stop to talk and catch up. To "greet one another," as they would put it. After exchanging a few words and pleasantries, they would continue on their way until they run into someone *else* they know, and then there would be more greeting.

You know what there wouldn't be? Any hurry at all. Because they know you'll wait for them.

Can you even imagine living in a culture like that? I can't. And yet . . .

There was *something* about the unhurried pace that my friend Adam found to be entrancing. He said that when he got rid of his watch, he did it thinking his new African life would be a boring one, full of waiting around. But what really happened flew in the face of his expectation—because the days seemed to go *faster*, not whizzing by at a hurried, frenzied pace, but instead at an enjoyable level. He would become so involved in a situation or conversation that he would suddenly realize the sun was starting to go down and think, *Wait. It's getting dark already?*

When you make room in your life to get slow, you make room for a *type* of living you never really envisioned.

Look, I know that scheduling, calendars, and planning are very necessary things; with all the traveling I do and the responsibilities I have, I would be lost without my calendar and my schedule. And I'm not saying we should all treat time as the Africans do. The tribal dialects of some of the people Adam worked with didn't even have a future tense. There was literally no way to talk about anything in the future in their language.

But when we strap on our schedule rockets and seize

the day with our preplanned itineraries, we very well may be missing some of the best, richest, most God-ordained moments out there. You can't live life on fast-forward.

Sometimes you have to push pause.

---

In some ways hurrying is genetic. It's buried in our DNA. Yes, we've elevated it to an art form in our technologically advanced society, but it's really been around from the beginning. At least as far back as Father Abraham.

I'm thinking specifically of a story we find in Genesis. Before Abraham became Abraham, his name was just plain old Abram; and God made a covenant with him and told him that he would have a bunch of descendants—that more people would come into this world through him than there are stars in the sky.

That's a pretty big promise, isn't it?

Especially because Abram—whose name at this point became Abraham—had no children yet. His wife, Sarah, couldn't have kids, so this promise from God was a pretty big deal. According to the numbers used in the Old Testament, Abraham was around seventy-six years old when this took place, which seems pretty old to be having kids—but whatever, it's the Old Testament. When we move on to the next chapter, we find out that ten years later Abraham and Sarah still don't have any kids.

Here's a question: Did God lie when He made that promise to Abraham about the star-numbered descendants? Of course He didn't! If God says He's going to do something, He's going to do it. But He's going to do it on His timetable, not yours or mine.

But Abraham got in a hurry. Or maybe he was just thinking he needed to help God along. Or maybe it was Sarah, thinking she was the problem and the reason they weren't having any kids. Regardless of the reason, Sarah suggested to Abraham that he sleep with one of her servants, a hand-maiden named Hagar. Maybe that's how God was going to build this family.

So he did it. Abraham married Hagar, then slept with her, and guess what—she got pregnant. Yay! Right?

Wrong.

Sarah got jealous as soon as she found out about the pregnancy and started mistreating Hagar—the Bible doesn't really say how Sarah went about that, so you'll just have to use your imagination. Tired of the poor treatment, Hagar took off and fled into the desert.

No worries, though, because an angel found her there and convinced her to go back. She was, after all, carrying Abraham's child, and Abraham had a promise from God that his descendants would be blessed and numerous. The angel also told her that her child was going to be named Ishmael and that he was going to be a wild dude who would be hostile toward any other brothers he might have.

Hagar, perhaps thinking that Ishmael would be her vengeance once he got old enough, headed back to the house where Abraham and Sarah lived, and everything went back to normal. At least, it was as normal as you can be when you have two wives and one of them used to be your wife's servant—whom you only married so she could have your kid, but now that she's pregnant with your kid it's causing all this tension and stuff—you know: normal.

A few months later, Ishmael was born.

Promise fulfilled, right?

Nope.

When Ishmael was about fourteen years old, God appeared once more before Abraham and told him the wait was almost over: the time was soon coming when he would have that long-promised son. God told him to name the kid Isaac; that He would turn him into a great nation; and that He would bless Ishmael, too, but that Isaac would be the one with all the juice, and all that. A little while later, some mysterious houseguests arrived and told Abraham that his son would be born during the next year, and lo and behold that's exactly what happened.

Abraham was now one hundred years old.

If you've been paying attention to the numbers I've been throwing out, then you'll realize that it took twenty-four years from the time of the initial promise to the time God came through on what He said.

If you keep reading the story, you'll find out that Ishmael created a whole mess of problems for Isaac later on down the road, and while he was blessed of God and all that, it's hard not to wonder what would've happened if Abraham and Sarah hadn't rushed to fulfill God's promise.

What might've happened if they'd slowed down—even to the point of waiting twenty-four years?

I don't know if I could do it. That'd be tough to have God tell me something that important—*you're going to have a kid!*—then to wait that long for God to bring it about. I would be tempted to try scrolling down to the end and helping God out, especially if it didn't look as if things were going the way they were supposed to.

Sure, waiting ten years is a long time, but it wasn't long enough.

Abraham, even after sitting around for ten years, still needed to slow down.

There's another part of the Bible where we can read a story about patience, and this time we'll find it in the words of the prophet Jeremiah, around a famous little verse that people love to quote.

I'm speaking, of course, of Jeremiah 29:11. If you're a Christian and you don't know the reference, you probably know the verse, because it's been *everywhere* the last few years: "'For I know the plans I have for you,' declares the LORD, 'plans to prosper you and not to harm you, plans to give you hope and a future.'"

This is a great promise that God gave to the Israelites in the midst of something called the Babylonian exile. Basically, the empire of Babylon, overseen by a king named Nebuchadnezzar, had invaded the nation of Israel, plundered it, and carried off its inhabitants to Babylon to serve as slaves. Remember the servant girl from earlier in the book, the one who told Naaman to go see the prophet to cure his leprosy? This was the same time period. The Israelites were completely destroyed by the way God had abandoned them to exile and were feeling pretty hopeless about the collective future of their nation—as well as their individual futures.

Then the prophet Jeremiah popped in, with all kinds of messages for the Israelites while they were in captivity, including this scripture. It is undoubtedly one of the more hopeful ones for the Israelite prisoners—God reaching into their world and saying, "Look, don't worry about this—I have plans for you and they're good. You're gonna like what I'm going to do with you. Even though things look really awful right now, I'm going to turn it all around for you."

I'd say that's pretty hopeful!

When we look at the other words wrapped around that verse, however, we can see that God's plans were more about the long term than immediate rescue. Because before He told the Israelites about their awesome future, He told them they needed to settle down in Babylon for a while. Build houses. Plant gardens. Get married. Start families.

*You're going to be here awhile. Seventy years, actually.*

Yes, Jeremiah 29:10—exactly one verse *before* everyone's favorite "plans for the future" verse—tells us God's time line for the Babylonian exile: "When seventy years are completed for Babylon, I will come to you and fulfill my good promise to bring you back to this place."

That's going to require some patience.

And notice what God told the Israelites to do in preparation for their escape from Babylonian captivity and triumphant return to Israel. Did He tell them to stockpile weapons for the big battle at the end? Did He direct them in one of our beloved training montages set to an upbeat rock song? Did He dump a bunch of books on them about unleashing the power of positive thinking or discovering untold blessings through the prosperity gospel?

Nope. He told them to relax.

*Be ordinary, you guys. Hang out. Do your thing.*

*Just wait on Me. Slow down.*

*There's no amount of hurrying that's going to change My plans, so you might as well just make the most of your time here.*

*I got this, so let Me be the Big One.*

*You go small.*

---

It's amazing what little kids can find in backyards. Stuff that we adults overlook because we've seen it all before, or maybe because we're taller and therefore higher and farther away from the interesting little things on the ground.

I think it's easy to get too familiar with this world, to the point of losing your sense of wonder at the marvels of God's creation. Have you ever seen a little kid—especially a toddler who's just learning about the way the world works—playing in an ordinary backyard? The outdoor space becomes a wilderness preserve, science laboratory, and bountiful playground all at once. Watch a kid turn over a rock, and see how engrossed they can get in the pill bugs and grub worms they find underneath. And you better believe they'll want to show you what they found, just because it's so *interesting*. In their minds, they think, *I've just discovered the most interesting thing in the world—I must share this valuable information and extraordinary experience with my parent or caregiver!*

They get so excited.

*Look at the intricate vein pattern in this leaf!*

*Look at this fly licking its fingers!* (Because that's what that looks like to a little kid.)

*Look at this cool flat rock!*

*Look at this cool lumpy rock!*

*Look at this rock shaped like a square!*

*Look!*

*Look!*

*Look!*

Kids know how to get slow. When kids are absorbed in play, when they are in the zone, they aren't worried about checking their e-mails or wondering if there's been any activity on their Pinterest boards. They aren't feeling a phantom *buzz* in their pocket, thinking that someone's sending them a text that must be read and replied to immediately. They aren't snapping photos of every waking minute while simultaneously wondering which Instagram filter they will apply to the finished product.

They're just hanging out. And they're full of wonder.

It's wonder-full.

What can we learn from them? How can we take our cues from the more innocent and less jaded among us, so that we can begin to incorporate some slowness in our lives?

Is this, perhaps, one of the aspects of *childlike faith* we hear so much about? When Jesus tells us we need to "receive the kingdom of God like a little child" (Luke 18:17), could He be hinting that this is part of what we need to do, to open our eyes to the wonder of it all, slow down, and revel in the ordinary?

And why don't we have slowness in our lives already? Is it because, deep down, we're maybe a little *afraid* of it? Do we fear boredom?

This is not a joke: I pulled up to a stoplight recently and looked both to my left and my right and saw that each driver was on their phone. Not *talking* on the phone, *looking* at it. Maybe they were returning a text message or catching up on their Facebook feed or playing a quick game of Words with Friends. I don't know. All I know is, they couldn't put their phones down long enough to sit at a stoplight.

That's just one instance I happened to witness at one of the thousands upon thousands of stoplights across the country, but does it say anything about our fascination with technology in the modern world? Have we forgotten how to get slow? Are we so determined to avoid boredom and ordinariness that we can't just sit at a stoplight and let our brains idle along with the engines of our vehicles?

This is getting tougher and tougher in our artificially lit

cities—seeing as there is such a thing as *light pollution* (do a Google search)—but when's the last time you wasted an evening doing nothing but looking up at the stars and letting your mind wander?

There's something magically ordinary about the middle of the night. Not staying up late to party or hang out with friends, but in the dark, early hours, when the rest of the house is quiet and asleep. Parents notice this whenever a sick child waking in the middle of the night interrupts the peace and tranquility. You stumble out of bed, do what you can to meet your child's immediate need, and then sit up with them to coax them back to sleep.

If you're a parent, then you've done this.

There's this mystical, wonderful sort of moment that settles on you once your child goes back to sleep. The baby gets a little heavier in your arms, or the five-year-old stops fidgeting on the bed and snuggles their face a bit deeper into their pillow. It's the ultimate in peaceful ordinariness, and if you take time to notice it, it feels holy.

In the midst of the moment, you want to stretch that feeling out for a few more seconds, even as you're ready to get back to your own bed and get back to sleep—after all, you have a lot to do in the morning. Because that *is* indeed a holy moment, a picture of the way God cares about you.

It's a way to get slow.

## Chapter 10

## GET INTENTIONAL

From 1992 to 1996 a city called Sarajevo, which was the capital city of the country formerly known as Yugoslavia, was under attack. At the time Sarajevo wasn't just the capital of Yugoslavia; it was also a European capital for art and music, a city that was known worldwide for its artistry and history of imagination, for creating beauty and order out of the chaos of everyday life.

But there were some rebels who wanted independence from Yugoslavia to create their own country, so they launched an attack on Sarajevo using every bit of artillery at their disposal: guns, mortar fire, tanks, rocket launchers, sniper rifles, and the like. Their goal was to bring the city—and the central government—to its knees so it would recognize their independence and superior might, and allow them to form their own country.

Inside the city were innocent civilians, people who just wanted to go about their business, who didn't give a rip about revolution or independence—who just wanted to live.

But they couldn't do that, because now they lived in fear of what might be coming from the hills surrounding the city— they never knew when a rocket or shell fired from a tank might explode next to them and destroy whatever building they happened to be in.

Nevertheless, the population of the city tried to carry on. Kids still went to school. People still went shopping. Artists kept performing.

On May 27, 1992, toward the beginning of the siege, a cellist named Vedran Smailovic was practicing in his apartment. As the principal cellist for the city opera, Smailovic had to keep up his skills, especially during a time of war. People needed music to help them cope with the hellscape their city was becoming.

While Smailovic was practicing, the war came to him.

Many parts of the city became unusable, reduced to rubble. Bombings were affecting businesses, churches, apartments. When a mortar shell or a tank blast leveled a bakery or a shop or a school, that bakery or shop or school went out of business. It was practically impossible to rebuild while Sarajevo was in constant danger of being bombarded again.

Supplies were limited or cut off entirely, creating even more shortages and scarcities. People who needed to do even the simplest things like buy bread from the few remaining bakeries in town stood in long lines to do so.

It was just such a line—formed to purchase bread at the bakery across the street from Smailovic's apartment—that

was struck by artillery fire from above while Smailovic prac-
ticed his cello. He felt the blast and, after the initial shock,
raced to his window to survey the damage. He was not prepared for what he saw—mangled bodies strewn in the street,
a tangle of people, bones, and bread. Twenty-two innocent
people, who had just been trying to feed their families, were
now dead.

Smailovic was enraged. He wanted to fight back in some
way, to protest against the violence that was destroying his
beautiful city. He wasn't a soldier, so he couldn't fight with
traditional weapons, but he *did* have an idea of a weapon he
knew how to use excellently: his art.

He was a musician; he would fight back with music.

And so in that moment, he began to formulate a plan—
a musical protest against the rebels, against the violence,
against the insanity he had witnessed.

Vedran Smailovic was going to get *intentional*.

He didn't wait; he started his protest the next day.
Donning the formal tuxedo he wore for performances at
the Sarajevo opera house, Smailovic gathered his cello and a
plastic stool and walked across the street to the pile of rubble
that used to be a bakery, to the killing floor of twenty-two
people, and sat down. He leaned his cello back on his shoul-
der, took his bow in hand, and began to play.

For this protest performance Smailovic chose a specific
piece of music. He played a composition called "Adagio in G
Minor," which had a history that only added to Smailovic's
protest. In World War II a bombing attack on the German

city of Dresden had destroyed fifteen square miles of the city center, completely leveling much of that city's art, culture, and antiquities. As the story goes, after the war a composer named Remo Giazotto found a scrap of paper in the leftovers of the city library, a scrap that contained only a few notes by a *different* composer named Tomaso Albioni. Giazotto decided to create something beautiful from the ashes of this bombing, and used those scattered notes as the basis for a composition called "Adagio in G Minor."

This was the piece that Vedran Smailovic played on his cello while sitting in the ruins of a bakery amid a war zone. A few notes from a different war, from a different time, from a different pile of rubble. A few notes that lived on, bringing beauty and serenity through the simple act of a bow, some strings, and a master cellist.

Smailovic performed this same piece in the same spot the next day. And the day after that. Every day he dressed in his tuxedo, took up his cello and stool, and walked across the street to play his protest.

For twenty-two straight days. One day for each victim.

Vedran Smailovic looked at a world being torn apart by bombs and guns and tanks and power-crazed leaders and decided he would *force* that world to acknowledge the beauty of life—the serenity and tranquility that come from a beautiful piece of music played beautifully.

He looked at what the world was trying to hand him and, using his cello, made a declaration for everyone who would listen: *This is not acceptable.*

Twenty-one years later, again in the month of May but this time in London, a completely different attack took place when two terrorists assaulted a British soldier named Lee Rigby as he walked down the street in the Woolwich district of southeast London. The men used a car to run down the soldier as he made his way down Wellington Avenue. They got out of the car and hacked Rigby to death with a knife and a meat cleaver, and then dragged his body into the street.

The two men intended to have a standoff when the police arrived, evidently planning to take out as many police officers as they could before being killed themselves. It was all part of a misguided plot they had concocted to create terror and subsequently convince British armed forces to withdraw from all Muslim countries.

In the midst of this, there happened to be a public bus trundling by the scene, and one of the passengers on that bus was a middle-aged woman named Ingrid Loyau-Kennett. Ms. Loyau-Kennett, an ordinary, concerned citizen who knew a thing or two about first aid, saw the body in the street, thought it looked like someone who needed lifesaving measures, and hopped off the bus to help. She knelt down, felt no pulse, and then realized the men who had attacked him were still there, eyeing her.

In that split second she had a decision to make. She immediately realized the severity of what was going on. She knew it was a busy area, that children were about to be dismissed from their school day and would soon be walking down that same street. And she knew that these men were unpredictable. One of them, she noticed, was carrying a gun.

What did Ingrid Loyau-Kennett do? She started talking to the men. She figured it was better to keep their attention focused on her—she was already in the situation anyway—instead of on any of the passersby. She asked what they were doing there, what they were hoping for, what they planned to accomplish—just let them talk and talk and talk. She remained calm and undeterred when one of them told her they were hoping to start a war in London. At one point she even tried to persuade one of the attackers to hand his weapon over to her, though he didn't take her up on the offer.

Eventually police arrived and, after some heated moments and eight gunshots, they were able to arrest the now-wounded men and take them into custody. Ms. Loyau-Kennett's bravery became a quick story on the Internet, as people rushed to tell the tale of an ordinary mother who confronted knife-wielding terrorists and backed them down until police could arrive.

When the situation got bad, she got intentional.

She leapt into action with what she had: knowledge of first aid, a conversational tongue, and listening ears—honed by years of being a mother.

It's a pretty crazy story, one I'm sure Ms. Loyau-Kennett will be telling the rest of her life. But while she was indeed brave, talking down terrorists will not be the crowning achievement of her life. No, that honor goes in a different direction. Because she's a mother of two, a former Cub Scout leader, a neighbor, a coworker, and just a human being living in a society.

The effect she has on her kids, on the other kids she was around during her time as a Cub Scout leader—that will have *much* further-reaching impact than the bravery she exhibited in the moment there in Woolwich. None of the other things, however, would get her on the news; but that's because they aren't really news. They're just too small of a story.

---

You know how I know God cares about the little things, and how He works in the ways we get intentional? Because I've seen it firsthand. Let me switch gears and tell you a family story about my son, Nolan, and our search for a Christmas car.

A long time ago, my wife, Jeanette, and I decided that Christmastime should not be just for our family but also for others. We wanted to be intentional in our approach to the holiday and show our kids that the idea of Christmas isn't about the presents they get or any of that ultimately inconsequential stuff. Instead, it should be about caring for others in the same way God cared for all of us by sending Jesus. And so, with this in mind, we started a thing in our family: when Christmas season rolls around, we do something nice for someone else—usually another family, if possible.

Come to think of it, we should probably do that at times other than Christmas too.

Anyway, as I've mentioned previously, my son, Nolan,

has embarked upon an acting career in film and television, and it's starting to pay off for him. He's been a guest star on a few different shows and has been in several commercials and movies. He even got to spend a summer in Iceland playing Russell Crowe's son for the movie *Noah*. It's been pretty cool to see the doors that have opened for him, and we'll see where it all leads eventually.

One of the things Nolan's acting career has led to is a pretty decent paycheck every now and then. He's not swimming in money, but he has more of it than most kids his age. And fortunately, he's not into spending money on stupid stuff like candy or little things here and there—he likes to save it and use it for big-ticket items, which we always make him pay cash for. Also, so that we can teach him a little about the importance of generosity, as well as teach him to trust God with his personal finances, we always peel off 10 percent of his earnings for him to give away in some form or fashion.

For Christmas one year, I had this idea that Nolan and I should get together and buy a car for someone. We live in Southern California, where public transportation isn't all that great or convenient or cost-effective. If you want to get around here, you really need to drive; but not everyone can afford to buy a car. I just knew there would be some family in our church that could really use a car, and what better way to bless a family in Southern California than by giving them a way to the grocery store, school, doctors' appointments, and all the other places a family needs to go?

Incidentally, Nolan is still too young to realize that different cars cost different amounts of money. In our family we drive a pretty new Toyota Prius, which isn't a luxury car or anything, but it cost a fair amount. When I floated this idea to him, that he should use part of his savings to contribute to buying a car for a family, his eyes went wide. He didn't think he had enough money.

"Nolan," I said, "the car *you're* going to buy for *me* when you're a rich and famous actor—that one will probably cost a lot of money. But that's not what I'm talking about. We could probably get a decent car for someone for two to three thousand bucks or so. It's not going to be the nicest car in the world, but it'll be *something*—a way for them to go where they need to go."

Once he heard that, his eyes went back to normal size and we agreed to split the cost of the car. Nolan would pay half, Jeanette and I would pay the other half, and since our daughter, Elise, is a dancer and has hardly any money, she would give sacrificially from her piggy bank and pay to get the car washed before we gave it away.

Well, we were excited. We even discovered that our church had a ministry specifically to pair people who might need cars with other people who could donate them. I called the church and talked to the person who headed up the ministry. They're used to people calling and saying, "I have this type of car that I don't drive anymore, do you have anyone who could use it?" And then they pair a person or family with that vehicle. They aren't used to having people like me call in and say, "I don't have a car yet, but I *do* want to give one to someone who needs it. Who should that be?"

Nevertheless, they agreed to my odd request, found the perfect family for us, and we were ready to go. The church set up a meeting for us to hand over the car on the Sunday before Christmas, in the parking lot of the church, at 11:00 that morning. Easy enough, right?

As I've mentioned, I travel a lot; and I wound up going out of town an unusual amount of time that Christmas season—a time of year that is just plain busy anyway. So with one thing and another getting in the way, it all came down to this: the day of the car giveaway came and we did not, as of that moment, have a car to give away yet.

Just a small oversight.

I wanted to follow through, however, on our original plan. I mean, after all, this whole thing was not only to bless another family but also to teach my kids about generosity and sacrificial giving, right? How could I teach them any of those valuable lessons if I didn't pull this off?

I got up early that morning and spent some time on Craigslist clicking on all the different cars for sale in Southern California, and most of them weren't that great. They were cheap, sure, but they were definitely not something I wanted to hand over to someone, even as a free gift. I wanted to do this right.

My research online led me to a guy who was located not too far away from where I live; he had, literally, *eight* different cars listed on Craigslist. At first I thought he might be a scam artist or something, but then I did some digging and found out he was legit. He owns his own business selling cars out of his driveway. Basically, whenever city or state governments want to get rid of a vehicle that they're no longer using, they sell them. This guy buys the ones with the lowest mileage, fixes them up a little, and then lists them on Craigslist and resells them for a good deal.

We went down there hoping for one of those good deals, but one thing I hadn't counted on when I talked to this guy—and one thing I noticed immediately when we pulled into his driveway—was that these cars were all old police cars! Every single car was white, with a giant black number decal stuck on the back or an enormous decal on the side announcing the California Highway Patrol. Some of them had both. Also, while they didn't have their sirens anymore, they *did* still have that bar thing separating the front seat from the backseat.

In other words, none of these cars screamed "Family vehicle!" at us.

Of the eight different cars this guy had for sale, only one of them was even remotely promising: a pretty standard sedan with a big number 26 decal on the side. I say it was promising because it was the one with the fewest stickers on it.

"Hey, man," I said. "Nothing in your ad on Craigslist said anything about these cars having all these stickers and decals on them. Do you have anything without this stuff?"

He brushed my concerns off with a wave of his hand. "Aw,

don't worry about it," he said. "This is all I have, but that stuff will come off with a little gunk remover. It's easy."

At this point we had only a couple of hours before our scheduled appointment to give away a car, and I didn't really want to spend those two hours scrubbing sticky goo off the side of the car. Whatever vehicle we gave, I wanted it to look nice when we handed it over.

And so it soon became clear after discussing things with this man for a little while that none of the vehicles he had for sale were going to work out for us—they just weren't what we were looking for. And at this point it was 9:30 in the morning. Just a mere ninety minutes before go time, and we still didn't have anything.

Fortunately, since we live in a rapidly advanced technological age, I was able to pull out my iPhone and hop back onto Craigslist to look for other options. While I was furiously scrolling online, Jeanette had a thought and suggested that Kias tend to be a fairly affordable yet reliable option for this type of thing. I thought that sounded great, so I started searching Craigslist for any Kia vehicles available in the general area between where we were and the church parking lot where we were supposed to be in ninety minutes.

I found one, and luckily it was nearby. It was also close to our price range. One drawback, though: it had 175,000 miles on it. Still, it was the best thing available, so I called the number listed in the ad and after a couple of rings, a man answered. I told him I wanted to buy his car right away.

"I'm on my way to church," he said. "Can we do it afterward?"

"Actually," I said, "we're on our way to church, too, and we're supposed to give this car to someone there."

He thought it over for a second, then gave us an address to a car lot and told us to meet him there in a few minutes. It looked like this was going to work out after all!

Before ten o'clock, we were standing in this man's car lot and looking over a white Kia that seemed to be a perfect fit. It had a nice clean interior, seemed to run great, and it was one solid color with no decals that needed to be removed. It was even already washed, so Elise was off the hook for her part of the deal.

The only thing that bothered me was the mileage—175,000 miles. That's a lot of miles for a car you'd hoped would be some family's dependable, reliable, everyday get-around car. It just felt like rolling the dice to give this car over to a family.

While those particular thoughts were going through my mind, I happened to look around and saw right behind me an ancient blue Buick. This thing was the complete opposite of cool—it was at least twenty years old, with four doors and fake wood trim along the outside that used to indicate luxury but nowadays just indicates a car is from a bygone era. It even had one of those pop-out cigarette lighters and an ashtray inside—that's how old this car was.

But there was something about it. Something I couldn't explain or really put my finger on—it just felt like this might be the one we were supposed to get. I pointed to it and asked the guy about it.

"Oh, someone donated that to me," he said. "You know, donated cars are the best, because they're usually from someone's recently deceased parents or people like that. The types of cars that just sit in a garage and never get driven or only get driven every now and then."

Well, *that* got me to thinking.

"Go look at it," the guy said. "There's not a scratch on it, and if you take a look at the odometer, you'll see that it only has 32,000 miles on it."

And *that* sounded *really* good.

"What are you going to do with it?" I asked, trying—and mostly succeeding—to hide my enthusiasm for what seemed to me to be the perfect car to give away.

The guy shrugged his shoulders. "I'll probably put it on eBay," he said. "Usually cars like that one, that are older but have really low mileage, they do really well online. It'll probably wind up being bought by someone who doesn't even live here—probably someone out of the country."

I took a moment to consider this old blue Buick, comparing it mentally to the newer white Kia. They both had their pros and cons, but I felt in my heart that the Buick was the car to get. I've been serving God long enough to know to pay attention to heart feelings like that when I get them.

"How much you want for it?" I asked.

He cocked his head sideways, gave me a price, and it was right around our target.

I looked over at Nolan, who seemed to be on board with this cool old car.

"We'll take it," I said.

And that was that—it was a deal. We did all the paperwork and got it smogged—which is a California thing. Because our air is so bad from everyone driving, you have to have your vehicle's emissions checked periodically to make sure your car isn't adding to the problem any more than any of the other cars are.

Oh, and this one was already washed too. Elise was excited about that part.

Once we had taken care of the details, Nolan and I hopped in to drive this old blue Buick over to the church while Jeanette and Elise followed us in our own family car. Since I was driving someone else's car, I didn't speed or break any rules of the road. I have to say, as I started getting a feel for this Buick, it was pretty awesome. Yeah, it was old-school, but it drove *great*. It felt more like driving a restored classic car than some junky old antique.

Oh, and best of all: it didn't have a police barricade installed inside it or California Highway Patrol written on the outside of it.

We showed up at the church at 10:55.

The family was already there, so they got to see us roll up in their new wheels. It turned out the family was a single mother with two younger kids, maybe a little younger than my own kids, and when they saw us pull up, they immediately did some little hops. The mother did that thing women do when they're crying joyously, when they put their hands over their mouth and nose. The kids clapped.

It was a pretty sweet moment, and not because we did this generous thing, but because *God* did this generous thing *through* us. We got intentional about our generosity, and then God honored that intention by guiding us through all the different potential cars to this specific one for this specific family at this specific time.

The story isn't over. I haven't gotten to the small part yet.

I stopped the car, parked it, turned the engine off, and then yanked out the keys and tossed them to Nolan.

"Why don't you hand this one off?" I said.

He smiled. "Okay."

We got out of the car and approached this mother and her two kids. The person in charge of the car ministry was there, too, but hung back so as not to be intrusive in this God-ordained moment. Nolan told the mother about how he'd been saving up his money, how he'd paid for half of the car, and how grateful he was to be able to give it to them. I'm not a very sensitive guy, and I refuse to admit that I *might* have cried, so let's just say there weren't very many dry eyes in the parking lot right then.

After Nolan told them our story, we got to hear some of theirs, which I'll leave out of this book in respect of their privacy. After learning the circumstances they were going through, Nolan and I definitely felt humbled that God had used us to meet a major need they had.

But here's the ordinary icing on this extraordinary

cake. While we were in the midst of talking, the younger of the two kids, a girl, leaned up to her mom and simply said, "I knew it!" And she said it in that way kids have—you know the way—when they have that confident air about something, which they saw coming from a mile away but had never articulated before. It's that ever-springing hopefulness kids have, that innocence that hasn't been squeezed out of them, drop by drop, by years and years of adulthood.

"I knew it, Mom!" she said. "I prayed about this, and I had a dream, and in the dream the car was *blue!*"

The mother gladly acknowledged her daughter, then turned to us. "That's all she's been talking about," she said. "That the car was going to be blue."

Boom.

Small.

God cares about the little stuff—the stuff that we overlook or find unimportant. This little girl wanted a blue car—and God gave it to her. Can you imagine what that did for her faith? How much bolder, stronger, and deeper her faith got in the instant when Nolan and I pulled into the parking lot and she saw this blue car coming toward her? What kind of impact did that have on the family—this girl talking nonstop all through the holiday season about how God was going to give them a blue car—and then He handed them a blue car?

As adults, we think having a new car *given to her* would be the important thing for this girl, but not so. A car? That's easy. God can do that, no problem.

No, this was something *really* amazing. *Truly* miraculous. This was a *blue* car.

Just like she'd dreamed!

After our time in the parking lot was over and the family drove away in their sweet blue Buick, we went to church as a family. But I didn't pay much attention to the worship or the sermon—I was too busy thinking about the little girl and her enthusiasm over their new blue car. I started wondering if there would be sometime later in her life, when she grows up and becomes an adult and inevitably loses that childlike wonder—if she would find herself in a place of doubt, and someone in her family would remind her of that car in all its blueness, and that memory alone would restore her faith.

God cares about small things like wonder.

We love to give God credit for the big stuff—for promotions or checks in the mail or free cars—those types of things. But sometimes it's the little things that make the biggest memories.

When we get intentional, we never know what might happen.

---

In these days of wireless Internet, when we stream our music online and get our television from a thick wire that runs from the cable company to our house, it's easy to forget about something as fundamental as the radio. But then we get in the car to head somewhere—across town or across the country—and the radio can become our best friend. Whether it's providing the latest news or the most up-to-date hit music or just a talk show about last night's basketball game, the radio is still woven deeply into the fabric of everyday life.

Have you ever been on a long, interstate road trip with nothing to listen to but the radio? It can be quite frustrating, because it seems as though you're always adjusting the tuner in order to pick up a station clearly. You'll be driving through a major populated area and finally dial in a nice clear signal of something you want to listen to, but then—as you keep going and leave that station's broadcast radius— the sound becomes obscured by more and more static, until it eventually goes away completely and you're forced to listen to something else.

That's not so bad, but it can *really* get frustrating when you're driving through the parts of the country that aren't as populated—which, if you didn't already know, is most of it. The United States has a large population to be sure, but it has a *much* larger amount of land that doesn't have many people living on it. And so you can go for long stretches— especially in the open-range West—with nothing but static on the radio.

I have a friend who used to be a long-haul delivery driver, and his territory was western Oklahoma, western Texas, all of New Mexico, and parts of Arizona. He used to joke that he could understand why the aliens crash-landed in Roswell, an especially remote part of New Mexico where the infamous Area 51 is rumored to be located. In his think-ing, they must've lost control of their flying saucer when they kept messing with the radio, unsuccessfully tweaking the tuning knob to find a radio station.

Here's one thing about radio that I find interesting: radio waves are always around us. Constantly. Wherever you're sit-ting right now, reading this book—whether you're at home or at work or in a coffee shop or waiting for your flight to leave at the airport or in the bathroom or waiting out the baby's nap—you are sitting in a simmering stew of *electromagnetic radiation*, part of which is made up of radio waves. You can't see them or feel them or hear them without the right equip-ment—more on that in a moment—but they're always there, always in the background, always waving around you, and they always have been, since the very beginning of time.

Don't worry—this isn't the same type of radiation as fallout radiation from a nuclear blast or the invisible stuff in a microwave oven that cooks the outsides of your food and leaves the inside cold. This is just background stuff that we don't ever notice, like the magnetic field or gravity.

Radio waves are just part of the universe—they exist here on earth, yes, but they also exist out in the farthest reaches of the universe. In fact, there are a couple of little robot cars driving around on Mars right now as I type this, and they talk to the scientists back here on earth using radio waves. We have other spacecraft flying through the solar system and they send back images and other data using those same radio waves. It's pretty cool, actually.

At some point someone figured out how to send information through radio waves, and they sent audio over the waves. It was a huge step forward for mankind, because it means that now I can listen to the All '80s Weekend while I'm running errands on Saturdays.

But that's getting off-track. The thing about radio I want to point out is that, while it's always there, you can't always hear it. In order to hear it you need two things: an antenna and a tuner. The antenna allows you to snatch the audio signals out of the air—the different stations and songs and music and political rants that get broadcast. But here's the interesting wrinkle: if you only had the antenna, then all those signals would be sent to your car speakers *at the same time*. You wouldn't be able to hear any of it because you'd be hearing *all of it*.

That's where the tuner comes in. The tuner breaks those broadcasts into their individual frequencies—so when you hear the deep-voiced announcer tell you "You're listening to 109.9 The Fish" on your way to Trader Joe's to pick up some roasted seaweed or dried mango slices, that *109.9* part is the station's broadcasting frequency. By the way, I made up 109.9—there is no such FM radio frequency; I did not make up "The Fish," because there *has* to be a radio station called that somewhere.

When you turn on your radio and push the buttons to adjust your tuner to a specific station, you are getting intentional about the sounds you put in your ears. You are making a conscious decision to listen to *this* station and, by default, not listen to any other stations. There are plenty of stations to listen to, all clamoring and crowding for your attention—so you use the tuner to find the one you respond to the most.

Hopefully you've stuck with me long enough and are now ready for the payoff to all this talk about radio waves and electromagnetic radiation. Because God's voice—His ordinary extraordinariness—is just like those radio waves. His majesty, His glory, His desires, His plans, His grace, His correction, His love—they're all there. God is *always* talking to you, always surrounding you, always desiring an audience with you, always looking to speak to you and tell you how much He loves you and wants to hang out with you.

When you get intentional about the world, you're tuning your internal spiritual radio to the God station, to His frequency, and letting Him inform your worldview. You're making a choice to focus on God's timing and His voice—which is very real and always worth listening to—and, by extension, letting go of the noise of the rest of the world. You're tuning out all the chatter and busyness that we call *ordinary*, and tuning in to what God would say to you. You're choosing His frequency in an effort to hear Him more clearly and let Him define for you what extraordinariness and success and big things look like.

That's what I'm talking about when I say you should get intentional. I'm talking about walking through this life with your spiritual radio tuned in to the frequency of the Holy Spirit and letting Him become the background music for your everyday world. And when a song comes on that you weren't expecting—whether it be a towering oak tree, or the wide-eyed awe of a baby looking at a ceiling fan, or the miracle of a dandelion growing through a crack in the sidewalk, or the crinkled smile of a random stranger—you stop what you're doing and *pay attention.*

That's intentionality.

That's living in the ordinary.

## Chapter 11

# GET BIGGER . . . BY GETTING SMALLER

There's nothing inherently wrong, I suppose, with wanting to do something big, especially when you want to do that big thing as a way to help grow God's kingdom. But I do wonder if we occasionally need a course correction to understand that we can get bigger by getting smaller.

Because the fact is, only a few of us are meant to do things that look big to everyone else, while *all* of us are meant to do things that look big to Jesus. And I don't know about you, but I'm way more interested in doing something for Jesus than I am for anyone else.

Let me illustrate this with a couple of stories, both of which took place at my kids' elementary school. One is about a talent show; the other is about soccer and clean classrooms.

First, the talent show.

I guess I should back up a bit and explain a little about my daughter, Elise. We've talked already about Nolan and his acting career, a part-time profession that puts him in front of people all the time. As a result he's becoming more and more used to performing—whether in an audition, or on a television or movie set, or in front of a camera for a photo shoot.

Elise? Not so much. She has no desire whatsoever to be in front of people, no desire to perform, no desire to go on auditions or any of that stuff. None of it.

You know what she loves? Dance. Not performing a routine in front of a crowd just yet, but everything else. That's her thing, and she can't get enough of it.

So you can imagine our surprise when Elise came home from school one day and told us there was going to be a school-wide, end-of-the-year talent show—and that she wanted to be in it. She had a dance routine she'd been working really hard on for a long time. It was a minute-long piece with a flip in it—that was a big deal for her—and all these other neat moves, and she thought she would like to perform it as part of this talent show.

"Really?" Jeanette and I said. "Are you sure about that? Because you'll be performing in front of all the kids in your school, plus all their parents, plus all the teachers. Have you thought this one through?"

We didn't want to talk her *out* of performing—not at all. We'd love for her to become a little more sure of herself, a little more comfortable being in front of others. But this notion of doing a dance routine in front of her whole school really seemed to come out of left field, so we wanted to make sure she felt confident. We wanted to put her in a position where she could feel that she succeeded.

She was sure; we signed her up.

The long-awaited day arrived and Elise was pumped up and ready to go. We dropped her off backstage and went to find some seats in the little performing arts center at her school. As we went in, a few students were standing at the entrance handing out folded pieces of paper; I took one, looked at it, and it turned out to be the program. Then I did a double take, because it listed every kid who was performing. And *that list was long.*

Forty-four kids long, actually. I counted.

*Forty-four kids!*

The entire spectrum of the school was represented in that program, with kids from first grade, sixth grade, and every grade in between. I settled in and prepared myself for what would become a very long afternoon.

Just as every other parent in the room did when they saw that program, I scanned the list, looking for my daughter's name. She was in a good slot, so Jeanette, Nolan, and I began to mentally check off each student as they came up to perform their talent. It was this seemingly never-ending parade of students who . . . well, let's be charitable and say that most of them were "overwhelmed by the moment."

There was a handful of the kids who were pretty good, but by far the majority of them were not ready for prime time. I mean, maybe some of these kids were really good at singing "The Star-Spangled Banner" in the living room at home, but most of them were incredibly nervous in front of the crowd, and it showed.

Regardless, the list of those who had not yet performed grew shorter, and finally it was time for Elise to get up there. I have to be honest—I was a little nervous for her, especially because she wasn't used to performing, and many of these other kids had wheezed out when it was their turn. But she proved my nervousness wrong, walking onstage as if she owned the place and brimming with confidence as she performed her routine. When she finished, she brought the house down. The place went nuts. It was great.

As we headed home afterward, I thought about what I'd just witnessed, about how many of those kids gave their part of the talent show some major effort but had not been gifted in the direction of performance. And the more I thought about it and talked about it with Jeanette, the more we began to get frustrated at how so many parents today are all about letting their kids "follow their dreams" without ever asking if those dreams are appropriate for their kids.

I'm not saying we shouldn't dream big.

I *am* saying that we should dream along with *God's idea of big*.

And sometimes God's version of big can look pretty small.

Let's go back to the school for the second story. The school my son and daughter attend is a charter school, meaning it veers a little from your standard public school experience. There are many different charter schools around the country, all with different emphases, but almost all of them have a requirement for parents: namely that if your kids are going to attend school there, you're going to have to volunteer some of your time to help run the place.

I have no problem with this. In fact I'm all for parents hanging out with their kids more, and if they can do it during the school day, then all the better. The cool thing is, our kids' school lets the individual parent take stock of what gifts and talents they have and put them to good use. And since one of my main talents is hanging out and encouraging people, as well as being competitive, I started looking at what they were doing for sports and recreation during recess.

It turns out that these kids would often play soccer while they were having their recess, but they played it on the hard, asphalt playground even though there was a grassy field nearby. I asked Nolan why they didn't go to the field to play, and he told me they didn't have anyone to supervise them if they went over there. There weren't enough teachers for one to watch the grassy field with the kids, nor were there any parent volunteers to do it at recess.

As soon as he told me that, I knew where *I* was going to volunteer.

I contacted the school and set it up—one day a week, I would show up at lunchtime and take any of the kids who wanted to play soccer over to the grassy field. This was great not only for the students because they got to play a real game of soccer on real grass, but also for me because I'm always looking for new ways to work out and I hate exercising in the gym. Running around on a soccer field for an hour sounded a thousand times more exciting than doing it on a treadmill.

I've been doing this for a couple of years now, and I have to say it's great. I really do enjoy it. Like I said, I'm getting in my workout for the day, so that's a plus. Beyond that—there's really no feeling like schooling a bunch of elementary school kids in anything, but especially in a frenetic game like soccer. They're just as competitive as I am, so we always have a fun, pretty intense match—though it just so happens that my team wins every week.

The teachers and faculty at the school have taken notice of what I'm doing, and they'll occasionally pull me aside and thank me for playing with the kids and all that, even though I didn't have to think twice about signing up for this as part of my volunteer hours. Why? Because I love it! It gives me a chance to get to know these kids and have some sort of positive impact on their lives, and it provides me the opportunity to be consistent.

Because of the ministry schedule related to my work with XXXchurch, I spend a lot of time flying in and out of churches. I come in on a weekend, speak to a congregation, shake a bunch of hands and hear a bunch of stories afterward, and then come back home. Don't get me wrong—I love it. I love that I get to make so many long-distance friendships with people from around the country and around the world. It's a part of my job that definitely has its benefits.

But by the same token, there is an aspect of routine and consistency that I miss; and that's part of what's so appealing about this little soccer game I have once a week at my kids' school. I get to be in this—with these specific kids—for the long haul. What sort of impact will that have? I don't know. Only God knows that, but that's not the point. The point is that by doing this small thing over time, I'm building, brick by brick by brick, something of real value with these kids. And I'm doing it while operating completely in my gifts.

While I'm out on the soccer field being noticed by the kids, the teachers, and the other parents, Jeanette is at the school too. She's there and she's volunteering, just like me. But you know what she's doing? She's cleaning.

Kids are messy. That may seem like a hilarious statement of the obvious, but I just want to reiterate it for a moment. Even at school under the structure of a classroom, kids are messy. Like, *super-duper* messy. They are experts at trashing classrooms—causing the garbage cans to overflow with paper, or getting their fruit-juice-sticky fingerprints all over their desks, or spilling the contents of their backpacks all over their storage cubbies. Kids can take a clean classroom and turn it into a disaster area in a matter of minutes, and all under the watchful eye of their teacher.

Jeanette goes once a week during lunch—at the same time that I'm out there kicking a ball around with the students—and cleans the classrooms. She straightens up books, vacuums, dusts, wipes down countertops, takes out the trash—the maintenance work that makes the difference between neatness and spotlessness. She's great at it, and she really makes the rooms much nicer environments to learn in.

You know who notices it? No one. You know who sees her doing it? Not a soul—because everyone is eating in the cafeteria or supervising all those classroom-dirtying children outside at recess. No one is inside to pay attention to my wife as she comes in and makes their world a little more organized. No one stops Jeanette in the halls and thanks her for the impact she's having on the future generation of leaders.

And you know what? She doesn't care. It doesn't bother her that she works in relative obscurity. She's perfectly fine not having a face-to-face impact on any of the students. She has no worries whatsoever about it. She loves what she's doing and is happy to volunteer her time in this way.

Because she's still—brick by brick by brick—building something of value.

Just like I am.

We are both building something big, and we're doing it by getting smaller.

Some of us have gifts that make sense in front of people, like my soccer playing.

Some of us have gifts that make sense behind the scenes, like Jeanette's ability to clean classrooms.

Both of these gifts *are the same in God's eyes.*

Looking back at that talent show, I get more and more fascinated because I think that too many of us—deep down—are interested in being "a star." Even my daughter, who ordinarily doesn't care at all about being in front of people, was drawn into the illusion of acceptance and success that performance offers. She doesn't usually have much—or any—desire to perform for an audience, but she still wanted to be on the stage, showing off what she does best.

And I don't think there's really anything wrong with that. I'm not saying kids shouldn't be given an opportunity to perform for others, and I don't want to rain on any of those parents' parades. These opportunities can be really good, building confidence in our kids and helping them to explore every possible avenue of their personalities so they can learn who they are and, by default, who they're not.

But I do wonder why we get interested in doing the big thing, in being the star of the show. You know who can really make or break a show? The backstage people. The ones you don't see. The small roles. The person who runs the sound, the person who operates the lights, the person who opens and closes the curtain or who pushes the scenery on and off stage.

We saw a lot of kids during that talent show, but you know who did the best job? It wasn't any of the singers, and it wasn't even Elise—sorry, Elise, when you eventually read this. No, the person who did the best job, who was most comfortable onstage, was the emcee. Yes, he was one of the students, but he interacted well with the audience. He put some life into the introductions when he read them, and he did his best to make the show entertaining while still making all the performers feel good about themselves.

He didn't try to be the star of the show—he just did his thing. He played his part.

And you know what? He pulled it off.

You know how many kids tried out for his job? You know how many parents were pushing their kids to be the emcee?

I think you probably already know the answer.

He wasn't afraid to get small, and by doing that, he was the biggest part of the show.

Let's take this discussion in a slightly different direction. I'm a big fan of the NBA, and I always think it's interesting how many people talk about the legacies of some of the greatest players the game has ever known. Sportscasters and fans like to rank players against one another, trying to determine with some sort of certainty whether LeBron James is better than Kobe Bryant, or whether either of them is better than Michael Jordan (which they are not). They usually break out objective numbers to do this, such as who won the most championships or MVP awards or scoring titles.

But you know who no one talks about? The athletes who won the most Sixth Man of the Year trophies. Role players and people who come off the bench don't tend to be celebrated; those players probably didn't go into professional basketball specifically to win the Sixth Man of the Year Award. They didn't spend their lives getting into the NBA just to contribute six points and two rebounds a night.

They all came into the game because they wanted to be the MVP. They all, at some point in life, had dreams and aspirations of growing up to be the biggest star in the league.

I think most of us can relate. Not only do we want to

do big things for God, but we're repeatedly *told* to do them by those in leadership positions in the faith. How many of you, like me, grew up with well-spoken cheerleaders for Jesus who encouraged you during your time in the youth or children's ministries at your church? Did they tell you that even young people can do great things for the Lord, and then proved it by quoting 1 Timothy 4:12 at you: "Don't let anyone look down on you because you are young, but set an example for the believers in speech, in conduct, in love, in faith and in purity"?

When we get caught up in a theoretical, arbitrary numbers game in the name of God's kingdom, we can lose sight of the importance of what we're *really* supposed to be about. I've had the privilege of starting many outreaches and ministries, and the types of things that get heralded and lauded in the media and online. But the more I've done it, the longer I'm around ministry, the more I've become convinced that God doesn't really care about our big thing.

God isn't interested in scoring titles or championships or Most Valuable Player awards. He doesn't want your actions or your efforts or your supposed bigness.

He just wants you. All of you.

He wants to take every single action, every interaction, every positive word spoken, every negative word held back, every kind gesture, every diligent workday, every soccer practice, every evening spent over a hot stove preparing a meal for your family, every quiet moment in between waking up and getting out of bed—all of it. He wants to take *all of it* and turn it into something extraordinary for His glory, defined by His terms.

When you truly allow this truth to wash over you, it's very liberating. It takes the pressure off of always going bigger, running faster, trying harder, and doing, doing, doing for God.

Instead, you just get to hang out with your Father and let Him handle the details. You get to do whatever He's put in front of you. Sometimes that will be a thing that impresses all your neighbors and Facebook friends and Twitter followers and members of the media, and sometimes that will be a thing that gets absolutely no buzz. It doesn't matter. Either way, you're following Him.

*Chapter 12*

# GET HUMBLE

We humans have had a little problem with pride—the opposite of humility—for quite a while now. One need only head to a museum to locate examples of humanity's self-importance, found in portraits, statues, elaborate grave clothes and markers, and monuments. In fact people will travel all over the world to see the narcissistic structures that kings, pharaohs, and various rich people have erected in their own names or the names of their loved ones—things like the Great Pyramids of Egypt or the Taj Mahal.

Take a minute to dig into your pocket or purse and find a coin. On one side of it you'll see the tails image, the details of which vary depending on the denomination of the coin. Could be a building, or some greenery, or something celebrating the wonderful achievements of one of the fifty states. But flip it over to the heads side, and you'll see the portrait of someone's head—hence the name *heads* (duh). This is just the way coins have always been—but do you know why?

It goes back to ancient times when coins were first

created as a means of making commerce fair for everyone across the board. Instead of having citizens trading lumps of gold and silver, the rulers of different empires started making coins that people could carry around with them.

The best part was that those coins would go to every corner of the empire, so they were a great way to get the message out regarding who was in charge and who wasn't. Therefore, you better believe the king or emperor or whoever was in power would make sure his image was on that coinage. And the instant there was a change in power—whether through revolution or due to a father handing down the empire or kingdom to his son—one of the first things changed was the money. Coins with images of the old emperor were melted down, and new coins were struck with the face of the new emperor on them.

This very well could have been what Jesus was referring to in Mark 12 when someone asked Him about paying taxes to the empire. Jesus heard the question and had the person pull out a coin. "Whose image is this? And whose inscription?" He asked. It was Caesar's, of course, so then Jesus said, "Give back to Caesar what is Caesar's and to God what is God's" (Mark 12:16–17).

In other words, this monument to Caesar's narcissism is pointless in the kingdom of God. You won't be needing this bit of portable pride where I'm taking you.

As Christians we can hear this and think we get it, even though chances are high that we still don't. I've known people who make their genius levels of humility a point of pride, sort of a "Check out how humble I am" type of thing. It's very easy for the balance of humility to tip into selfishness. In fact there is an ongoing argument among philosophers about whether true altruism—an unselfish concern for others, giving to them for their benefit and not yours, that sort of thing—is even possible. Some would argue it isn't, because as soon as you help someone out who needed it, you feel a sense of accomplishment or—look out for it—pride. You feel good about yourself, which *could* be the motivation for your kindness, which would negate the not-for-your-benefit part of it.

But I'm getting off-track.

I've found one thing that really keeps me humble is community. Living in intentional community with others is a must if you're going to retain any amount of humility, because you're surrounding yourself with people who can discover who you really are—and love you anyway.

Jesus knew this and did us all a favor by modeling community for us. Jesus was the biggest thing in traveling ministry that we've seen before or since. Everywhere He went He drew these enormous crowds that would follow Him around and keep their eyes peeled for miracles. Jesus did crazy stuff like healing people with terminal diseases and pulling large amounts of food out of thin air.

If anyone had a reason to find excuses to be alone, it was Jesus.

But Jesus wasn't like that. He went out of His way to spend time with twelve guys, His disciples, doing life with them and showing them what He was all about. Jesus would tell parables to the assembled crowds, then break the stories down for His disciples after everyone else had gone back to their homes.

He was the picture of accessibility and humility, especially when it came to being in community with His disciples. Look, I'm just going to be blunt now. I've been all over the United States and the world, and I've been in more churches than I can count; and some of the pastors of these churches do *not* act like Jesus acted toward people. Some of these rock-star pastors rope themselves off from the people in their congregations, hiding out in a secure back-stage room until it's time to preach. Then they head back to the room and have a security guard escort them to their car so they can drive home in privacy. These guys aren't accessible—they're the untouchable CEOs of their own personal brands.

*Jesus wasn't like that.* He went out in the crowds. He spent time with the people, and when He was done with that, He spent time with His disciples. He made sure to surround Himself with community and in so doing maintained a sense of humility within that community.

Plus, He used the community of disciples to teach us exactly what we need to know about finding humility in our own world. Just check out what He said to two of His disciples, James and John, when they got into an argument with the other disciples about who got to sit next to Jesus in heaven. James and John went to Jesus and asked if they could sit on either side of Him, and when the other disciples heard about it, they got extremely mad—creating a major ruckus among this small community of devout believers.

That's when Jesus laid down the law, and told us what we need to know about finding humility—as well as what He thinks about those inaccessible rock-star pastors:

> You know that those who are regarded as rulers of the Gentiles lord it over them, and their high officials exercise authority over them. Not so with you. Instead, whoever wants to become great among you must be your servant, and whoever wants to be first must be slave of all. (Mark 10:42–44)

You want humility? Serve others. As disciples of Jesus, you're called to put aside the brainless opinions of the high officials and rulers. It's almost as if Jesus is saying, "Look, these guys in power, they think they're something special and they show it by pushing other people around just to show that they can. If you want to be like that, you can do it, I guess, but it's kind of stupid, you guys."

Instead of chasing after power, Jesus tells us we need to chase after humility. *Real* greatness, *true* bigness, *honest* extraordinariness come through the easiest thing in the world: service.

Humility is its own form of greatness, and it's a greatness that far surpasses any of the piddly greatness as it's defined by those who have no concept of the kingdom of

God. So if you want to be great, then serve. And you can start by serving the others around you, like your family, your coworkers, the people you rub shoulders with on the street or in the store. And just in case the disciples might have thought Jesus was telling them—and, by extension, *us*—to do something He Himself wasn't about, He followed up that statement with this: "For even the Son of Man did not come to be served, but to serve, and to give his life as a ransom for many" (Mark 10:45).

Jesus was the Ultimate Servant.

In our modern, post-Enlightenment, emotion-obsessed culture, it's easy to draw a line of connection between humility and low self-esteem. Often we think those two things are interchangeable, where, in order to be humble, you have to think you're not that great of a person, or be down on yourself, or always hanging your head in a fog of self-loathing. Not so! Do you think that describes Jesus, the guy who was the most gracious, most giving Servant the world has ever seen? I sure don't.

I look at the Gospels, at the character of Jesus, and I see a Man who was full of life. Who took a keen interest in every person He met, who was so immensely popular and charismatic that He drew enormous crowds, even as He taught things that were apparently contradictory to what most of those good believers had heard all their lives. Jesus wasn't a macho man, brash and arrogant, but He also didn't shrink away from crowds or attention (or from a fight over what mattered—grace and the kingdom of God).

Jesus was the very definition of humble—a person who seemed more interested in other people and only in talking about Himself when it pointed people to the grand scheme of what God was up to.

He was a servant.

And He showed us humility by staring suffering in the face—because there was no greater suffering than what Jesus endured on the cross—and embracing that suffering as part of His service.

You want to be humble? Serve.

You want to stay humble? Embrace suffering.

Now, before you accuse me of saying something I didn't say, let's stop a moment to think this through. I'm not saying that we should go out of our way to seek out suffering—that won't make us humble. If anything, that has the potential to make us proud of all the challenges we can endure and turn us into some sort of suffering addict. What I *am* saying is that, when we acknowledge the fact that suffering exists—that there are days that are just plain crappy and that sometimes people we love make bad choices or that this world has not yet been fully redeemed and the kingdom of God, while at hand, is not yet completely established—we learn a thing or two about humility.

Here's another aspect of humility we can draw from Jesus' words in the Gospel of Mark: an understanding that our acts of service are all about Him and have nothing to do with us. What do I mean? I mean simply: *God doesn't need your ministry idea.*

His plans aren't going to come crumbling down if you don't do your thing.

God's kingdom is not contingent on *you*. Or me. Or any of us.

Does He use our works? Absolutely.

Does God want us to partner with Him in bringing about His plans and purposes for this world and all the individual people in it? You better believe it.

Does Jesus *need* you to do your part? No way.

Think about it. If Jesus needed you to do something, then you'd have some sort of sway over Him, wouldn't you? You could hold Jesus' feet to the fire. It would make Him powerless to act unless *you* let Him do it. He would be saying, "Come on, man—I just *really* want to do this great thing in this person's life, but I can't do it because you aren't doing what I told you to do."

Do you really think that's how this whole thing works? I don't.

I think God is God and He's going to do what He wants, while respecting the choices we all make. If someone makes the choice to send their life spiraling down into a depressive haze of drugs, porn, and high-fat foods, God is going to allow that person to do that. This is the *free will* part of the world He created.

And when that person's horrible life choices affect other people in their world—their spouse, or their parents, or their kids—God's going to work in those situations too. Maybe not in the ways we expect Him to, and not on the timetable we'd always want, but He *does* work. He *will* do His thing.

God is all about redemption sooner or later, and He will bring it. If you're in the midst of suffering as a result of choices—be they your own or someone else's—please understand that I'm not dismissing those or even saying God brought them on you. You can trust Jesus even in the midst of that.

I'm saying this for those of us who are tempted to think we're a big deal, who pastor a megachurch or who write best-selling books or who head up a well-known, well-regarded international ministry that helps people stop using and making pornography. When you get in the spotlight—even a small one—you can be tempted to think the spotlight exists for you. That you did something to earn the recognition.

That it's about *you*.

And if it's about *you*, then God must be impressed, right? He must be all, "Man, I sure am glad Craig Gross is doing what he's doing."

Which is true.

But then we can tack on a little extra to make it *un*true. We can add this thought from God: "Thanks, Craig. I couldn't have done it without you."

Boom.

Not true.

Everything I've ever accomplished in ministry is something that God could've done without me. He doesn't need *me. I need Him.* I need to use my gifts and callings and talents for God's kingdom, and I need to use them because it adds to *me*.

Remember when we were talking about the garden of Eden a few chapters ago? Remember how God told Adam to take care of the garden? That's what I'm talking about here— it's laughable to think that Adam could do anything that looked like actual work. His responsibility wasn't to keep all the plates spinning as a favor to God, to help God out of a jam. No, God gave Adam that job in order to help *Adam*.

If you have kids, you already understand this instinctively. Haven't you ever been doing something around the house when your young child volunteered to *help* you?

"Can I help you vacuum the living room, Mommy?"

"Can I help you blow the leaves off the roof, Daddy?"

"Can I help set the table?"

"Can I help?"

If you've ever encountered this from your children, you have probably taken delight in the help. Not because your kids *actually helped you*. It's highly likely that they probably *haven't* helped you at all. In fact they may have made your job a little harder or more time-consuming. Sometimes accepting the offer of your kids' help gets in the way of your schedule, because you know it's now going to take *longer* to wash the car than it would if they'd just stayed in the house.

The job would get done whether your kid helped or not. Their overall contribution to the cleanly swept kitchen floor was to stand around holding the dustpan, then to set the dustpan down by the pile of dirt, then to spread the dirt around with the dustpan, then to let you sweep the dirt into the dustpan, and then to empty half the contents of the dustpan back onto the floor when they tried to pour the dirt into the kitchen trash can.

What are *you*, as the parent, getting out of this help? In a practical sense you're not getting anything—except maybe more work.

But at the deeper, richer, parental level, you're getting a profound sense of delight in watching your child as they feel their accomplishment. They haven't really *done* anything, but man, are they sure proud of the little they've done. "I helped you!" they'll say.

Sure you did, kid.

And you'll smile, beaming from ear to ear, not for the work they've done, but for the heart they had all along.

I think that's how God feels when we do stuff for Him. It's really all His work—He's just delighting in us, reveling in the opportunity He gave us to "help Him out."

You see what I mean? God doesn't *need* us any more than you as a parent *need* your kids to crack the egg into the bowl of unbaked brownie mix—and leave behind any pieces of the shell.

When we grasp this, we begin to grasp the essence of humility. And we can have a ball, helping God bring about His kingdom. We begin to understand the passions God has given us and start to put them to use for Him, not so we can *do* something but so He can delight in us.

And that's humility.

## Chapter 13

## GET LOW

Like any other long-term married couple consisting of two opinionated, vocal people, my wife, Jeanette, and I have gotten into our share of fights over the past fifteen years. Married couples can be madly in love and still fight, whether it's about important things—money, raising the kids, a major job transition—or unimportant things—what you're going to eat for dinner, whether you should buy those new shoes for the kids, what kind of laundry detergent you should use. Come to think of it, we've probably fought over all those things and more.

But one thing Jeanette and I had never fought about before was prayer.

Until we did.

Here's how it happened.

In 2007 we felt the Lord was calling us to transition our ministry base from Grand Rapids, Michigan, to Las Vegas, Nevada, in order to start a new phase of the XXXchurch ministry—which would eventually become Strip Church.

We started months of planning and doing all the massive amounts of busywork you have to do in order to pull off a major cross-country transplant like that. We made several exploratory trips out to Vegas to figure out where we were going to live and do ministry, and on one of those trips, we started looking around for housing.

No, this was not when we had the fight.

After visiting a few different places, we showed up to a property with a host of soon-to-be-built condos for sale. They had a model home up that was just ridiculously awesome and right up our alley. We loved everything about it—we loved the place itself, the location, the idea of living in an apartment building. This was going to be great.

We were sold. We took the money we'd gotten from selling our previous house—which was no small amount of change—and made a down payment with the plan that this condo would become our new home in Vegas, even though it wasn't technically built yet. But it was supposed to be finished soon. Within a year. Which was fine, because that roughly fit our timeline for moving.

We flew back to Grand Rapids and got down to finishing our time there. It was great and we finished strong, but before long it was time to officially move to Vegas. But there was a little hiccup, because our condo wasn't yet ready for us when we arrived—and it wouldn't be ready for probably another couple of months.

Still no fight between Jeanette and me. It's coming, though.

In addition to the condo for our family, we had also rented a two-bedroom apartment for some interns who had made the trip with us to be part of our Vegas work. So we figured we could live in that apartment with our interns—it would be a little cramped and uncomfortable, but we'd done stuff like that before and could get by for a little while.

Picture this: you have our family of four, Jeanette and myself and our two young kids, *plus* four interns—all living in this apartment. It was inconvenient, and we were always in each other's business, but we made it work.

It was only going to be for a couple of months anyway.

Shortly after arranging this living situation, we did a walk-through of our condo and picked out some of its amenities—you know, the colors to paint the walls or the faucets to install in the master bathroom. The place was probably close to 90 percent completed. It just needed the finishing touches, but we couldn't move in yet. So we were going to have to wait.

The apartment we had rented happened to be near the location of our new condo building. Every day, at least twice a day, we would drive past that condo. And every time we drove by, the kids would start chanting from the backseat, "Build our house! Build our house!"

By now it was October 2008, and the big economic collapse had just happened—so in addition to being only *almost* finished instead of *all the way* finished, our condo was rapidly losing value. Even so, we didn't care about that aspect of it; we just wanted it to be completed so we could get out of this apartment arrangement and have some of our own family space again.

At this point I was beyond fed up with the way we were living. I was done waiting, so I said to Jeanette, "We could get a full house for less money than we're paying for this condo. What do you think about saying, 'Screw this,' and getting a house?"

Nope. Still no fight.

She considered the idea, and had a few questions about my idea—the first and biggest one being, "Well, what about our deposit money? You think we can get it back?"

"There's no way," I said. "We signed a contract, and if we back out, we'll just have to walk away from that money and hope we can make a better investment somewhere else. We'll have to scrape together a down payment from somewhere, but that's better than living like this."

"Okay," she said.

I did some digging and found our original paperwork, which included the address for the company handling the financial aspects of the condo purchase. I sent a letter telling them we were frustrated with the lack of construction on the condo and that we wanted to back out of the purchase. Then I went up the road not too far from where we were living and found a pretty nice house that was a far better deal than what we'd gotten ourselves into. Again, this was the economic collapse of 2008, so people were panicking and were just happy to have someone looking at the property.

Around this point in the story, as we prepared to buy

this house and move into it, Jeanette casually mentioned to me, "I'm praying that we get our money back."

Now. Now is when the fight happened.

Because I, just as casually, said, "I'm not sure God cares about us getting our money back."

And that stopped her in her tracks. "Wait," she said, getting serious and a little bit mad, "what do you mean?"

"Well," I said, "I guess in the big picture of things, this money doesn't matter much to God. It's just money. I mean, yeah, it's a lot of money, but it's just money, you know? Why would it matter?"

"Why *wouldn't* it matter?"

"Because *big* things matter to God," I said. "You know, our ministry does, our move to Vegas did, having kids did—those are things that *matter*. Something like this? I don't think it does, especially because it was our choice to walk away from the condo. We're not walking away because God told us to; we're walking away because we don't want to do it anymore."

She narrowed her eyes at me and thought for a moment. Then she squared her jaw and said, "Well, I'm still praying."

In situations like this I can get snarky—it's not a good quality, I know, but it's part of who I am and something I'm working on—and that's exactly what happened here. "What's God going to do?" I asked. "Send a miracle or something? Put a basket full of money on our front porch?"

"I don't know," she said.

"Like, what's your prayer exactly?" Yes, I'm the big, smart Christian preacher guy, and I'm digging in on something dumb like this, as if Jeanette needed a perfectly worded prayer full of specific action steps in order to force God to get our money back. I can get really dumb sometimes.

"I'm just praying that we get our money back."

Stupidly, I kept pressing the issue, and that's how we got into a major—and mostly unproductive—discussion. We argued about what God cares about; about the differences between big things and small things and whether that even matters to God; about prayer in general and what you should and shouldn't "believe for" when you pray; and about why you should even pray at all.

One thing that might help you understand the reason for our opposing viewpoints in this argument is the difference in our backgrounds. I grew up in church, doing all the churchy things and learning all the churchy words. I memorized Scripture and heard sermons and knew all there was to know about every possible scrap of evangelical theology. I had marinated in the stuff all my life, so I thought I had a handle on all this.

Jeanette, on the other hand, grew up outside the church. Her parents didn't take her; she wasn't around it, so she didn't know anything really about what went on inside churches. She couldn't speak the lingo and wasn't fluent in Christianese like I am. She came to Christ when she was nineteen years old, then promptly went to Bible college. She didn't have nearly the *wise experience* of someone like me, and so, in my deluded way of thinking, she had to have been completely wrong.

After our long-ranging discussion—okay, it was a fight—
we came to a truce and started to move forward. Jeanette
was going to keep praying if she wanted to, and I agreed not
to make fun of her for it.

The next day we did what we did every day and went into
town, and that, of course, meant driving by our condo building. And as we did, instead of hearing the kids chant, "Build
our house! Build our house!" I heard Jeanette start chanting,
"Give us our money back! Give us our money back!"

Cute.

This went on for a few days. Until they put up the fence.

We'd had easy access to the building before this. We had
gone inside several times to check out the progress of our
condo, to see what they'd gotten around to doing and what
they still had to do. But now there was this fence around the
building, and no way for us to get in.

That seemed wrong. And off.

What was going on? I called the construction company to find out exactly, and I got the answer we expected:
the downturn in the economy had put a major stoppage
on home buying, and that included people buying condos,
meaning the property developer hadn't sold enough of
the condos to finish *building* them. The guy was flat out
of money, and the economy wasn't going to come roaring
back anytime soon.

It sure looked like that money was gone.

Even so, Jeanette kept on praying, kept on chanting,
"Give us our money back!"

Just for the record: Jeanette and the kids were doing the chanting in fun. They weren't doing some kind of voodoo mantra to actually have an impact on the spirit world. This wasn't an incantation or any sort of New Age feel-goodery— it was just a fun way to remember to pray.

And wouldn't you know it, we got a letter in the mail from the property developer not long after that fence went up. And in this letter, we got the story on what was going on with our condo. The letter said that our deposit had been sitting in an escrow account ever since we'd made it, and that if we wanted to give up our condo and get back the deposit, we were welcome to do just that.

They wanted to mail us the check.

Jeanette and I wanted to go pick it up in person.

I'll never forget the look on Jeanette's face when she saw that check. It wasn't a smug, I-told-you-so kind of look— though she would've definitely been entitled to that. It was a look of peace and serenity. It was the look of a kid who knows her Father has got her back.

For Jeanette that check was a symbol that God cares about *every* part of our lives, working His grace into every situation, even when we get ourselves into messes.

For me that check was a lesson, and something changed in me that day. I began to realize I don't know everything about God, and that my concept of big things and little things needed to be redefined.

And it was all because of prayer.

Prayer is probably the biggest component for going small to serve a big God. Why? Because nothing could feel more ordinary than whispering a handful of words under your breath as you go about your day—driving to the store, riding the train to work, rolling out of bed in the morning, laying your head down at night—and then knowing that God heard those words and can move heaven and earth on your behalf because of them.

Look, there are hundreds and hundreds of books on prayer, not to mention several shovelsful of Scripture about it, so I'm not going to turn this chapter into a meditation on why we should pray or a point-by-point rundown of the theology of prayer. If you've read this far in the book already, I take it that you're already on board with prayer as a concept.

What I *would* like to talk about, what I think are the most important parts of prayer *as it pertains to this topic*, are these two things:

THING 1: *How* we pray

and

THING 2: *What* we pray for

Let's talk about the *how* first.

Here's how you pray: you converse with God.

That's about it.

Okay, let's look a little closer.

Prayer is not an incantation. Prayer is not a thing you

say to magically make God do something or not do something on your behalf. Prayer is not a perfect string of words you put together that forces Jesus to go to work for you.

Prayer is just hanging out. Talking to God, telling Him about what's on your heart or your mind. Asking Him to help you or to give you wisdom or peace or patience or willpower or whatever. And then listening to whatever His response might be.

Talking and listening. Both of them, equal sides to the coin of prayer.

When you pray, you don't have to turn it into a big production in order to impress God. I don't know where we got the idea that someone who is an eloquent speaker has an in with God when it comes to prayer, while someone who can't string a complete sentence together is going to be a failure. That's nonsense.

You can pray wordy, paragraphs-long prayers. You can pray short, two-word prayers. You can pray loud prayers. You can pray quiet prayers. You can pray by yourself or you can pray with a group of people—I recommend healthy doses of both. You can pray at any time, at any age, in any language. It doesn't matter who you are or where you are—you can pray.

You can pray from your own heart and spirit, trusting the Holy Spirit to give you the words you need as you need them, and you can also borrow already-written prayers from the Bible or from a prayer book.

You can pray in solitude in your bedroom or out among the crowds.

You can pray with your actual breath or you can pray silently to yourself.

You can pretty much pray anywhere.

The only time you *cannot* pray is when you *do not* pray.

Let's move on to Thing 2: *what* we pray for.

One of the unfortunate side effects of the self-awareness that came from the Enlightenment is that we started to think in terms of ourselves. In other words, we started seeing the world through our own eyes, as if we were the most important things in it. And, if left unnoticed, this thought process can trickle into what we pray for. Namely, we tend to pray for *us*.

God wants to hear about our concerns, most definitely; He doesn't want us to limit ourselves. Because when we can take the focus off ourselves and start to pray for others—be they family members or friends from church or someone you saw on your Facebook feed or a ministry you believe in or the heads of your government or any other random person you hear about in the news—you start to broaden your world a little bit. You step outside of the Box of You and see there's a great big world out there that you get to be part of.

You get to pay attention to the small stuff.

I don't know if you've noticed this before, but when Jesus gave us the Lord's Prayer, He showed us not only what to pray for but also that prayer is a communal activity. In other words, He didn't give us a singular prayer that is meant for me alone or for you alone. The text of the Lord's Prayer doesn't read, "Give me today my daily bread" or "Lead me not into temptation but deliver me from the evil one."

No, it's about *us collectively.*

Yes, it's fine and great to pray for yourself. I do it all the time. Every day. But we are missing out if we keep the focus there.

One more thing about what to pray for: prayer is not just a time for you to dump your thoughts, feelings, and requests on God, and then check out. Prayer is a time for you to *communicate* with God, to have a conversation with Him. Have you ever been at a dinner party or backyard barbecue or after-church greeting time and gotten into a one-sided conversation with someone? It starts off okay, but then it gets really, really annoying really fast and you start to think, *Wow, this person is really wrapped up in himself.*

When you pray, don't be the only one talking. Take time to listen! God wants to use your prayer times to tell you things—about yourself, about Himself, about His plans for you, about His incredible love for you. He could talk to you all day and still not get even remotely close to giving you a taste of the never-ending banquet that is His love.

The other great thing about prayer is that you can listen to God anytime. Remember a few chapters ago when we were talking about God's voice being like a radio station you can tune in to? Think of your prayer time as making time to pay attention to what's coming out of the speakers. Because when you do that, prayer time can be *any* time. When you're doing the dishes, when you're mowing the lawn, when you're stuck in traffic, or you're at the airport waiting to board your plane.

Prayer is an incredibly extraordinary force that transforms this world into God's definition of ordinary. And that is something to pray about.

*Chapter 14*

# A WRENCH IN THE WORKS

If you looked closely at the cover of this book, you might have noticed underneath my name the phrase "with Adam Palmer." Adam is a friend of mine who has helped me in some respect with almost all my books as an editor, a researcher, and sometimes a writer. If there's a story in any of my books that has to do with history or literature, he's probably the one who found it.

Anyway, while Adam was doing some work on this very book, he got involved in an incident that, I think, makes a nice bookend to what we've been talking about. With his permission I'm going to tell it here.

It was a Saturday morning, and Adam was heading to a neighborhood coffee shop to do some work on this book. We were getting close to an internal deadline for completing the manuscript, so Adam was pulling some crazy hours to get it finished, including working on a fine summer Saturday morning. As Adam prepared to leave his peaceful neighborhood, he noticed a strange gold Nissan sedan with a flat tire parked across the street, a short distance from his house; and hard at work changing the tire was a young woman, by herself.

Adam put his stuff in his car, got in, and drove over to see if the woman needed any help. But during the few seconds between the time when he first saw her and the time when he got to her car, she had started walking down the street, apparently out of frustration. Assuming she was on her way somewhere—perhaps to a friend's house or the home of a nearby relative—to get assistance with her flat tire, Adam drove away.

*Probably for the best,* Adam thought. *I do have a deadline, after all.*

While on his way to the coffee shop, Adam's wife, Michelle, called him on his mobile phone.

"I'm out of coffee at the house," she said. "Do you mind bringing me some real quick?"

*Sure thing, not a problem.* Adam popped into the coffee shop and got Michelle a cup of coffee to go, doctored it just the way she liked it—as the Beastie Boys once put it, she likes "[her] sugar with coffee and cream"—and brought it back home.

As he pulled up in front of his house, though, he saw that the young woman with the flat tire was back, and she had another woman there to help her. So he had dodged a bullet—Adam could drop off his wife's coffee and get back to the book. Except as soon as he got out of his car, the helpful woman saw him, pointed to his house, and asked, "Do you live there?"

Hesitant, he replied, "Yeah."

She pointed to the hubcap that was covering the flat tire. "Do you have a tool that can take this off?"

*Aw, man*, Adam thought. But then he remembered he was working on a book specifically about this very thing—finding God in the ordinary, small things of life. If he couldn't recognize this little deed that he could do to help out a stranded motorist—and then do it—then he had kind of lost his authority in what he was trying to communicate. The irony of the situation—that he would give up an opportunity to do a small thing in order to go work on a book that encouraged people to look for opportunities to do small things—wasn't lost on him, so reluctantly he walked across the street to have a look.

Upon inspection he noticed that her Nissan had those giant chrome wheels, the kind that require special ultra-thin tires and that have a complicated system of screws and nuts to keep the wheel in place. He examined the hubcap covering the lug nuts and noticed that she needed a hex wrench, also known as an Allen wrench—one of those small L-shaped pieces of metal that come with bedroom furniture you have to assemble. Having assembled many, many pieces of furniture for his large family, Adam had plenty of these wrenches.

"I think I have something that'll work," he said to the helpful woman, while the young stranded driver stood looking on. "Lemme run inside and check."

Adam went into his house, handed off the coffee to Michelle, and explained the situation to her as he went down to the basement to search for the appropriate tool. He found a collection of hex wrenches that he'd inherited at some point, then took them back outside to see if one of them would fit.

He found one, and after quickly removing the hubcap, the changing of the tire was under way. But the victory party didn't last long, because the driver didn't know anything about having the appropriate wrench for removing lug nuts—those are the big screw-things that actually bolt the wheel to the car.

The helpful woman asked the driver if she had a wrench that might match the lug nuts on her car, and the driver didn't really seem to have an answer. The trunk of the car was packed with all kinds of nonsense—an infant car seat, a skateboard, bags of stuff—so the driver just started pulling everything out and dumping it on the street in search of a wrench. The helpful woman went to her car to look for one, and Adam went to his car as well to dig out the lug wrench that comes with every vehicle. He got it and took it over to the Nissan to try it out, but it didn't fit. Same with the lug wrench that the helpful woman had in her car.

"I can go to the auto parts store down the street," the helpful woman—let's call her Diane—said, "and see if they have a wrench that would fit your wheels."

The driver wasn't really paying attention, but she mumbled, "Okay."

"So I'll be right back," Diane continued.

More mumbling from the driver as Diane walked

toward her car, which was parked along the curb, just down the same side of the street as the Nissan.

"You can just hang out here while you're waiting," Adam told the driver. "Get out of the heat. I have to go do some work, but you can hang with my wife."

"Your wife like jewelry?" the driver asked. She hooked her thumb around a gold chain necklace—one of several she was wearing—and raised it to show it to Adam. "You wanna get her a necklace?"

"No thanks," Adam said, already trying to figure out various ways to get back on schedule and get back to the book.

Right around the time Diane drove away toward the auto parts store, Michelle came outside to see how things were going and invited the driver to have a seat underneath the tall maple tree in their front yard. Adam began to explain to Michelle the plan about waiting for Diane to come back, but as he talked, the driver kept interrupting the conversation by pulling random items out of her purse and asking about them.

"Do you need a DVD?" she asked, holding up the faces to two separate car stereos. "I got two."

"No thanks," Adam said, ignoring that she had just referred to CD players as a DVD and trying to get back to his explanation to Michelle so that he could get back to work.

"Do y'all know what this is?" she asked, now holding up a compact plastic cube.

"That's an iPod dock," Michelle said. "You can hook an iPod up to it so you can listen to it without headphones."

"I ain't got an iPod," she said, then went back to rummaging in her purse.

Adam and Michelle exchanged the knowing glance of a long-married couple, and Michelle expertly changed the subject. "Would you like some water?" she asked.

"Yeah!" the driver said, brightening up.

Michelle went inside to get a glass of water for their unexpected guest, and Adam followed her into the house, leaving the driver sitting under the tree in their front yard.

"What have you gotten yourself into?" Michelle asked when they were inside.

"I have no idea," Adam said. "I thought they just needed a wrench."

"Something's not right here," Michelle said. And it was true. Something was indeed not right, to the point where Michelle—who is as hospitable as a person can be, who always has an open door policy for just about anyone—felt very uneasy about welcoming this woman into the house and decided to leave her instead under the tree in the front yard.

Michelle and Adam went back outside to deliver the water—and a bowl of grapes Michelle had quickly put together—only to discover that the driver had vanished. Her car was still there, and her purse, keys, and mobile phone were on the ground under the tree, but she herself was nowhere to be seen.

Adam got the feeling he would not be working on the book that morning.

Puzzled, they looked down the street to see if she was

walking again, but she wasn't anywhere. Adam even jumped in his car and drove around the neighborhood looking for her, but she had simply disappeared.

When Adam got back to his house, Diane had returned and was busy at work changing the tire. He went over to tell her about the driver's mysterious disappearance, and Diane shrugged. "She left her stuff?" she said. "I guess that means she'll be back. Let's just change this tire and then she'll be ready to go when she gets back."

"Sounds good," Adam said.

"It's a good thing you showed up earlier," Diane said. "We didn't know what we were going to do about that tire—I was just going to give her a ride to her house."

"Yeah, no problem," Adam said. "Happy to help."

Diane stepped aside to let Adam do the dirty work of changing the tire, which he dove into. He was focused on the tire when he heard Diane welcome back the driver; apparently the woman had just gone for a stroll—she had, after all, not been very present in any of the conversations that had been going on about her. She seemed to Adam as if she was in another world, and, even though it was now ten o'clock in the morning, he began to suspect she was either high or drunk.

Nevertheless, he got the tire changed and announced to the driver that her car was now good to go. But he was concerned about her ability to drive, so he asked her flat-out, "Are you drunk right now?"

"No, no, sir," she said hurriedly. "I'm sober. I'm just stressed out."

And without a word of thanks or gratitude, she got into the car to drive away. She started the engine, revved it, and then sat there, as if trying to figure out where to go or what to do or even how to drive. Meanwhile, Adam and Diane stood on the sidewalk to let her leave, and that's when they both noticed, for the first time, the *other* flat tire.

The car had two.

Adam and Diane waved her off and told her about the other flat. They explained that she would need to be towed, then started running down the various options with her. In the midst of this Adam noticed a police car driving down the street and past his house. He tried to flag the car down, thinking a police officer might be able to assist this now much-more-stranded driver, but the officer took no notice of Adam's gestures and kept driving.

The stranded driver got out of her car, and the trio of them just sort of stared at the other flat for a while. She really wanted to drive on it, but Adam and Diane let her know that would be a bad, bad idea—she wouldn't get anyplace where she could do anything, and she might be a safety hazard to other people on the road.

They were talking through some other options when a second police car drove by slowly, this time turning onto Adam's street. Adam again tried to flag down the officer, and it seemed to work. The car slowed down as it went past, and it looked as if the officer was going to help after he parked down the street a short distance.

Adam walked down the street to talk to the police officer

and tell him what was going on, but when the officer got out of his car, he walked *away* from Adam and toward the house of one of Adam's neighbors. Adam looked a little more closely and saw that the first police car he'd seen was now parked in front of that house, and some of his other neighbors were gathered in the front yard and talking to the police officers.

And then the pieces of the puzzle clicked into place: the mysterious disappearance of the driver; her persistence in trying to unload the stuff in her purse and around her neck; her unfamiliarity with the stuff in the trunk or how to drive the car.

He'd inadvertently been helping to fix the getaway car of a house thief.

Adam jogged the few feet to where the neighbors and police officers were gathered. "What's up?" he asked, already knowing the answer.

"There's been a break-in, sir," said one of the officers.

One of his neighbors piped up, telling him that they'd seen someone leave the house of their next-door neighbor, who was away at work that morning. Adam described the stranded driver to them. "That was her!" they said.

Adam never did get back to the book that morning. Instead, he saw the police arrest the driver, then saw her run from them—hands cuffed behind her back—when they tried to put her in a squad car, then saw them chase her down and get her in the car, then saw her slip out of her handcuffs and *run again*, then saw her get captured *again* and cuffed hand-and-foot, then saw her sitting in the front yard when his neighbor came home and found some stolen items inside the Nissan—along with lots of items stolen from other houses—and then saw the driver get taken away to jail for committing a rash of burglaries.

It was definitely a crazy Saturday morning.

But here's the point of this story, or the *key*, if you will.

What happens if Adam follows his original plan and gets some work done on this book?

What happens if Adam doesn't help when Diane specifically asks him for help?

Here's what happens: Diane drives this thief home, and she gets away.

But instead, Adam helped out—begrudgingly—and wound up unknowingly detaining a serial burglar long enough for police to arrive and arrest her.

Hopefully you've seen by now that it doesn't take a whole lot to start a chain reaction leading to big things.

Sometimes one small act can change the entire course of a day or a neighborhood—in Adam's case, it was agreeing to find a wrench.

Sometimes it takes a lifetime of small acts to do the big thing.

Sometimes it takes a community of people—like Adam, Diane, and Michelle, as well as the police officers and eyewitness neighbors—to bring some justice into the world.

Sometimes it takes just one.

Sometimes justice—or peace, or calm, or triumph, or joy—can seem miles away.

Sometimes they feel as close as your fingertips.

My encouragement would be to not sweat that stuff.

Let God be God.

He's up to something. All the time, in every way, everywhere on earth, God is up to something; and He's inviting you to get ordinary and have a part in it.

You don't *have to.*

*You get to.*

You get to have a part in God's kingdom by being ordinary.

Small.

Which is huge.

---

Shortly before my last book, *Open,* was set to release, my publisher came to me asking for ideas for my next book. I had a few vague thoughts in mind, but on the whole I was pretty stuck.

So I got in touch with Adam Palmer and asked him for some ideas that we could work on together. He shot off a few, but one that we both responded to really strongly is what wound up becoming this book. Here's what he said in that original e-mail:

> Basically, as a member of Generation X who grew up in event-driven youth ministry, I was told my whole life to do "big things for the kingdom," setting up an expectation that I had to go build some huge ministry or get a bunch of

notches on my belt for all the souls I personally converted. I spent much of my twenties alternating between a driving passion to do something "big" and a guilt-ridden malaise because what I was doing wasn't "big" enough in my mind. And I don't think I'm the only one who has felt this way. So what I'm thinking is, can we encourage people that God doesn't do things on a scale that looks "big" to us? That living a seemingly ordinary life can, in fact, be extraordinary from God's point of view? And how liberating would that be, to counter all the messages of being "radical"? I'm not saying that we don't do crazy stuff or that we live safe, comfortable lives—I'm saying we need to redefine what we consider to be ordinary, and that the simple life of the "ordinary" Christian could have just as much impact on God's kingdom as the Porn Pastor does.

Well, I read that e-mail from him and flipped out.

As you have now read, that's pretty much exactly what we talked about in this book. So if you enjoyed reading it, you have Adam to thank for suggesting it in the first place.

But as we were finishing it up, I started thinking about how interesting it was that Adam came up with this idea in the first place. Because he's been around and working with me for a long, long time, and most of the time, he doesn't get any credit for it. Outside of a couple of books, you won't see his name on most of the projects he does, because as a writer, editor, ghostwriter, or whatever other role he takes on when it comes to the printed word (and he performs

those roles not just for my books, but also for XXXchurch
.com and many other things you may have read), he's almost
always in the background.

I'm in my element when I'm onstage in front of a group
of people, or talking with a reporter in front of a television
camera. Those are places where I thrive, because that type
of communication comes easily to me.

But I'm not naturally a writer. I can get my thoughts
out through a keyboard, yes, but usually they're misspelled,
grammatically incorrect, and are often missing punctuation and capital letters. So I need people like Adam who will
not only help me get my thoughts down on paper but who
will also clean up those thoughts, organize them, and add to
them in a substantive way so that people like you can read
them and understand what I'm trying to say.

Which is why I find it interesting that the idea for this
book came from a guy who has almost always taken a backseat on a lot of projects, but who has also worked really
hard to make sure they got out the door when the deadline
arrived. And yet, while Adam's in the backseat, I'm up here
in the front seat, pitching a book to a publisher about the
small things—and then writing it.

This book went through several phases before it got
into your hands. Originally we called it *Ordinary God*, but
that wasn't really setting the marketing department at the
publisher on fire, so it morphed into *Everyday God*, but
there was already a book with that title. So it became *Small
Stuff Matters*, and then it turned into *Better Than Big*, and

we sent tons of e-mails back and forth trying to come up with the exact title that would help everyone know in an instant what we're trying to say.

Why the difficulty? And why am I being so transparent about this process? For a couple of reasons. For starters, I think the refreshing message that you can embrace the ordinary parts of life is kind of a tough sell. We've covered that territory already, but I do find it interesting that so many of us want to buy books or attend seminars or conferences that promise to help us get ahead in life. As if we can just uncover the secret formula, then we'll be all set.

But the thing about faith is that *it's faith*. There are no rules for success. There's no formula. It just is. It's just hanging out with God, following Him wherever He goes, and being content in Him and not in ourselves.

So yeah, giving you permission to relax is kind of a bold move for me—and for my publisher.

As for the transparency part, I'm giving you this behind-the-scenes look at the compilation of this book because I learned things while working on it that I was not expecting to learn.

I've come to find that most people aren't going to start national movements or grow nonprofit organizations to major levels. Over the last several years, as I and the rest of the XXXchurch team have built up our ministry, I've started working more and more with people in the nonprofit world; and all that time spent around those people and those organizations has made me a little jaded.

Maybe *jaded* isn't the best word for me to use. A better word would be *regulated* or *adjusted*, like how the water in the swimming pool is too cold when you dive in, but spend a little time in there and your body gets used to it. When you're around a bunch of type A go-getters that tend to get drawn to the start-up nonprofit world—people who, not coincidentally, are very similar in personality to yourself—you start to think that everyone's the same. That everyone is just like you and has the same perspective on life as you.

This is such an easy trap to fall into, especially when you are surrounded by people who share similar passions. I was once at a conference in Las Vegas specifically geared toward people like me, people who like to start up nonprofit organizations in order to make the world a better place. XXXchurch had a session, and everyone who came to it had different ideas—many of which would be very cool should they come to pass.

The energy in that room during our session was intense and amazing. So many people getting excited about all these different ideas, each of us thinking of great ways to help each other turn those ideas into action. It's invigorating, walking alongside creative visionaries as they take their first steps toward implementing their ideas.

I sometimes get so excited about some of the ideas I hear—and the potential existing within them—that I really get behind the people who have those ideas. Over the years I've given up days at a time to work with someone on their vision, and more than once I've let people live in my house so they can do nothing but focus on the important job they have to do for the kingdom of God.

That stuff comes naturally to me. I don't think of it as work—in my mind it's fun—because that's just how I'm wired. It's the way God created me.

But the longer I've worked on this book, and the more I've thought about it, the more I've started to realize that there are *way more people* in this world who are *not* like me, who don't find energy and excitement in getting ideas off the ground, who have no entrepreneurial bent whatsoever.

If you *are* wired like me, to go big, then sure—do that. Be true to who you are and who God made you to be. But if you're not—and I know you're out there—then you still have a part to play in establishing the kingdom of God here on earth, and that part is *just as important as mine.* You are just as important as any of the other self-starters and go-getters and big-goers that you see or know.

But here's the big lesson I learned while working on this book: for those of us who are wired like me, now is the time to understand that the small stuff matters as much as the big stuff.

I originally approached this book as a way to tell people who aren't like me that they were okay, but I was still coming at it almost from a place of pity. Like, in my mind, I thought the people who would learn something from this book were the people who weren't fortunate enough to have my skill set and natural, God-given abilities. Since those are mine, I just assumed they're the best.

But once I started digging into this topic, the more and more I thought about it, the more I realized that this book was as much for me as it was for the people I originally thought would benefit from it.

Let me explain. As I was working on my previous book, *Open*, my grandmother passed away at the ripe old age of ninety-one. My grandma and I were real close, but she had been sick for so many years that by the time she passed it didn't have much of an impact on me. People my age sort of expect that their ninety-one-year-old grandmothers will pass away at some point soon. But there was still a vague sense of loss and an even vaguer sense in the far, far back of my head that someday I, too, will be joining my grandmother in heaven.

I dedicated *Open* to my dad and said in the dedication that I wanted him to be the first one to read it. My dad never read the book, and he passed shortly before its release. But unlike my grandmother, who got to ninety-one, my dad only made it to seventy. That was the biggest shocker about my dad's death—how quickly it came and how relatively young he was compared to my grandmother when it happened.

Besides my own father and grandmother, I've only had one other person close to me die—a woman named Marie, a friend who lived in a retirement home whom I'd met on the side of the road when I was much younger than I am now. You can read about that story in one of my previous books, *The Gutter: Where Life Is Meant to Be Lived.*

I've been a healthy guy most of my life. I've never broken

a bone, never had major surgery, never gotten so sick that I had to spend the night in a hospital. Any bouts with illness I've had were your garden-variety cold or the flu or stomachaches or sinus infections. I don't have to take prescription medications to regulate my heart or my stomach acid. I don't even have to wear glasses. I've been remarkably fortunate to sidestep the worst that sickness has to offer.

That all changed while I was working on this book.

It all changed in an instant.

As I said before, I travel a lot to speak to different churches and at different events. I had flown to Texas and checked in to my hotel to spend the night before speaking at a men's breakfast the following morning—one of XXXchurch's Porn and Pancakes events. So I was just hanging out in my hotel room, watching *SportsCenter* and getting mentally ready for the talk I was going to give the next day (even though I've delivered it so many times I probably could do it in my sleep), when my head felt like it suddenly exploded. Shooting pain radiated throughout my head, like lightning had struck it or someone had put it in a gigantic vise. Yes, I know those two things don't really go together, but my head hurt so much it felt like it was blowing outward and pressing inward at the same time. Eventually the pain became so intense that I thought I was having an aneurysm or something, and I took the drastic step of telling my friend Dave, who was in the room with me, to dial 911 so I could be taken to the hospital.

The ambulance arrived and off I went to the emergency

room. They rushed me in, looked me over, performed all sorts of tests, and determined that I was not actually in the process of dying, and that—as far as they could tell—I was physically normal. They kept me there to keep an eye on me and to wait for some test results to be sure, but their best guess was that I was fine.

The pain in my head had been subsiding while I waited in the hospital, and between the time I left at 4:30 that morning and the time I spoke at the men's breakfast at 7:30, I was pretty much back to normal. Nothing else out of the ordinary happened the rest of that day, so I just chalked it up to some out-of-the-blue health anomaly and flew to my next destination, eventually making it home.

A couple of weeks later I was in Las Vegas to catch up with my friend Jake Luhrs, who was performing at Vans Warped Tour.

We were in the taxi on the way to dinner after his show, and once more my head exploded—figuratively, of course—but this time I started to feel faint. Though I was trying to talk to Jake and communicate what was going on, he later told me that I was pretty much incoherent and that nothing I said to them made any logical sense.

Once more I found myself in the emergency room after a call to 911, for the second time in as many weeks. Once more I went through a battery of tests at the hands of expert and well-meaning physicians. And once more I was told there was nothing wrong with me physically.

"However," they told me, "when you get back home to

Southern California, you should visit your regular doctor and have them test you to see if you have multiple sclerosis."

That sure isn't what I wanted to hear, but I really wanted to get to the bottom of this recurring mystery. So when I got back home, I set up an appointment with my doctor and subjected myself to more tests than I knew they could dream up. And after those came back inconclusive, I subjected myself to even more tests. And then more. And then even more.

All told, I spent roughly two months being poked and prodded and strapped into machines. I got an EKG, an EEG, an MRI, an MRA, a stress test, a test for seizures, a spinal tap, and had enough blood taken out of my veins to fill a swimming pool.

And at every turn, I was told I was fine.

Then came the time for my wife and kids to head out for a little vacation getaway. We were in the parking lot at the airport when another headache struck me and practically knocked me out, and this time I threw up out the window. Instead of getting away we got ourselves to a doctor. We wound up using the time we'd scheduled for our vacation as a time to get more tests done, trying to get to the bottom of the mystery of what exactly was wrong with me.

One of the many specialists I went to see was a neurologist. He told me, "You just have a headache."

"No," I said, "this is more than a headache—this is something way worse."

He tried to write me out a prescription. "Just take this medication and you'll be fine," he said.

But that wasn't good enough. I wanted to know *why* I was having a headache pretty much every day for two and a half months, and *why* that headache would occasionally turn so severe that I couldn't do anything or function in any productive way.

I didn't get that prescription filled. Instead I went to more specialists. I went to a rheumatologist and a cardiologist and a whole bunch of other -ologists, and all because I knew there was *something* affecting my head negatively. I wanted these people to get to the bottom of it.

The last straw came a few weeks later in Phoenix, Arizona. We were there to spend some time as a family with friends of ours, and celebrate our daughter Elise's birthday. While we were having a birthday party for her, another headache overwhelmed me; but unlike all the previous unexplained pain, this sensation was different because I also felt it in my chest.

We all got in the car and my friend Ryan drove me to the hospital, doing his best not to panic while in the driver's seat, with me crumpling up in pain in the passenger's seat. The pain was so great that I wasn't very aware of my surroundings, but I did overhear one of my kids ask Jeanette, "Is Dad going to die?"

Here's the thing: ever since my kids were old enough to know anything about me or make any observations about their dad, I've tried to show them that I'm strong. *Dad is the leader. Dad is in charge. Dad is going to take care of you.*

And now they thought I might die.

And honestly? I wasn't entirely sure they were wrong in their concern.

We did our best to assure them that I was going to be okay even though we were completely in the dark as to what was going on.

I was in the hospital for two days and nights, once more being subjected to more tests and procedures, once more being told by all the doctors and support staff that they didn't know what was wrong with me.

By this time my publisher was about to release *Open* and I was scheduled to do some publicity and promotional tours to help get the word out about it. Even though I'm used to traveling, this kind of traveling can get pretty exhausting. I wasn't sure I was physically prepared to pull it off safely.

I had been booked on a flight to New York City and had a few possible interviews lined up with major publications and television programs, but I still didn't know for sure whether I should go. I debated both sides very seriously all the way up until an hour before my flight to New York was scheduled to leave, and I decided that I should indeed go.

My travels to New York City went off without a hitch, healthwise. I was only in New York a few days to make some appearances and do some interviews. The Anthony Weiner "Carlos Danger" story was just blowing up at the time and affecting his campaign to become mayor of New York City, making it a perfect subject for the Porn Pastor to weigh in on while I was in town.

I also managed to connect with an old friend of mine who lives in Manhattan and has a thriving career in the media. I got to know this guy through some of the interviews and media attention we've gotten through XXXchurch, and though I'm not in New York City very often, whenever I'm there we try to get together. He extended his friendship to me years ago, and I was absolutely shocked this guy would make such a generous offer of his time and his relationship to me.

My friend was about fifty years old at the time. A very successful media professional who has won probably every award you can win in his field, he's rubbed shoulders with rich, famous, and powerful people. He has sat down with presidents, pop stars, and other influential newsmakers, and yet manages to remain extremely grounded in his perspectives on his life and the role his work should play in it.

Also, he's a devout believer who loves Jesus like crazy. So you can imagine that I not only have respect for him as a professional member of the media but also as a fellow Christian who just happens to have wisdom dripping out of every corner of his soul.

We connected while I was in New York City, and he invited me for dinner one evening while I was in town. While I was having dinner with my friend, the subject of my health came up and we got into a lengthy discussion about what was going on in my head and the rest of my body. I described in way more detail all that I've just laid out for you here in these pages, and my friend listened intently to all I had to say.

When I was finished, he took a deep breath, looked me in the eyes, and said, "I think I know what's going on."

Finally! This guy has talked to tons of people in all sorts of industries and professions, so I was certain he was going to be able to pass on some information to me from some health professional he interviewed once.

I leaned forward in my chair until I was barely making contact with it. Now I was going to have some answers, some knowledge that none of the very competent and intelligent medical professionals I had seen previously could impart to me.

"Craig," he said, "you're not going to like what I'm about to tell you, and I know that because you're a lot like me. You do a lot of great things, and you lead a lot of great people in a wonderful mission, but you work so hard that I think what I'm about to tell you is going to be hard for you to hear."

*Uh-oh.*

"I could be wrong," he continued, "because I'm no doctor, but you just told me about every test you've taken and every doctor and nurse you've seen in four different states, and every single one of those tests and doctors has told you there's nothing wrong with you. So maybe, just maybe, all your physical symptoms are your body's way of giving you a warning."

"A warning?" I said. "About what?"

"I think your body is trying to get your attention, and I think it's so you can be reminded of a scripture in one of the gospels, in the book of John, chapter three, verse thirty."

Here's what that verse says in the New King James translation: "He must increase, but I must decrease."

That's it. It isn't hard to memorize, but man, is it hard to get a handle on.

My friend continued speaking along those lines. "That is such a powerful verse of Scripture," he said. "It's so powerful, and yet people like you and me have a difficult time believing it, don't we? Don't you and I tend to think everything revolves around what *we* do next?"

I had to nod in agreement because he was definitely right. Even after I'd done all the work on this book recommending *specifically the opposite of this*, I realized in that moment that I still believed it. I didn't just *read* this book—I *wrote it*, and I was still thinking big, big, big.

"Maybe," my friend said, "your body is telling you that you need to slow down, and maybe even stop for a while to let other people around you carry the torch for a season. Maybe you need to let someone else keep things going for right now. Maybe all these instances with your health, these headaches and chest pains, are a sign for you to step away and take a backseat in your ministry."

Maybe.

"Maybe," he said, "you need to see what the Lord is capable of doing through your ministry—but without *you* in the front seat."

Well, he was right—I did *not* want to hear that. Being in the backseat and slowing down are not part of my personality makeup at all. I'm a doer; I'm a go-getter. I'm not a sightseer. When I travel to other cities for speaking engagements or to do publicity for a book, I spend most of my downtime in my hotel room working or dreaming up the next new adventure.

In a lot of ways I don't even know *how* to slow down.

In retrospect what was really interesting about the counsel my friend gave me was that he didn't know I was working on this very book at the time. In fact, while I was with him Adam was putting the finishing touches on the first draft because it was due to the publisher in the next fifteen days (we obviously added this part after the fact).

In the moment of hearing my friend's wisdom, and especially that passage of Scripture, "He must increase, but I must decrease," I didn't even connect the dots to this book. Because I thought I was writing a book for people who aren't like me, I thought I was trying to tell people something along the lines of, "You don't have to start something, but you can go play a part in other people's stuff."

And the whole time I was saying that to others, I was sitting on this side of the line thinking, *Yeah, but it's much more fun over here.*

My problem was that I didn't know what it was like to be part of the small things, to really take time to notice the everyday things that God delights in, the little bits of life that He gets excited about.

Because He *does* get excited about them! And I was missing it!

He must increase, and I must decrease.

That night my friend Ryan, who had traveled to New York City with me in case I needed any sort of medical assistance while I was there, met up with me after my dinner with my wise media friend and asked how the evening had gone. Now, I'm the type of guy who almost always leads with my mouth. I don't have much of a filter, and I tend to just tell people what I think—sometimes whether they've asked me or not. In other words I don't often process things before I speak or give an opinion on them. So you can imagine Ryan's shock when, after he asked me how dinner was, I told him, "It was good, but let me sit with it."

And that was all I said.

That's not me.

Later that night I was talking with Jeanette on the phone, and when she asked me how dinner was, I said the same thing to her: "It was good, but let me process it for a couple of days before I talk to you about it. We can discuss it in detail when I get home."

That's *definitely* not me.

I finished up my media appearances and went back home to Southern California to see my wife and kids. During that whole time, I just sat with this conversation. Especially the John 3:30 part of it.

I sat with it on the plane.

I sat with it on the ride back to my house.

I sat with it as I embraced Jeanette and the kids when I arrived at the door.

I sat with it as I went to bed that night.

I sat with it over the next couple of days as I went to five more doctors and got five more tests and was told with authority and finality that, sure enough, I was great on paper and that there was nothing wrong with me. And so it finally began to sink in to my brain that there *really was nothing wrong with me*. Not physically, anyway. Because if there really *was* something within my body that needed to be fixed, they surely would've found it by now. I would have found a treatment, or a cure, a medicine, or a pharmaceutical trial that could fix it.

That's what I wanted to do, but I started to realize that doing any of those things would prevent me from working on—and fixing—the *real* problem.

Me.

Maybe my friend in New York City had been right. Maybe all this physical stuff really *was* my body warning me, or the Lord using my body to warn me, that I needed to slow down.

See, I'm the kind of guy who does not easily declare defeat. I pretty much believe that every question has an answer, and that if I just work hard enough and look diligently enough, I'll find that answer. I will chase after a solution as hard as I can. That made this continued health scare all the more frustrating for me, because the longer it went on and the more evidence I got, the more elusive the answer became. I was chasing an answer, but I wasn't sure I was even headed in the right direction.

So it was initially difficult for me to hear what my friend

had to say—the answer was *myself.* And I had to determine whether that answer was one I could trust, because it was going to require a pretty dramatic lifestyle change for a while.

That's why I had to process it for so long. It took awhile for the idea to gain traction in my heart and mind that I already held the key to my problems in my hands—and I'd been holding it the entire time but hadn't been able to recognize it.

The more I thought about it, though, the more I came to discover that I had to decide whether I really believed God when He said I had to decrease so He could increase.

The only option for treating my health concerns, the only thing that made sense, was to trust the Lord.

I reconsidered my own priorities and positions. And I realized that while I'd been writing this book for others, I'd also been unknowingly writing it for myself. This message isn't for a certain *kind* of person—it's for all of us.

God has given all of us gifts. Me, you, everyone. He gives different types of gifts to different kinds of people, but there is no escaping the fact that you have them. Sure, your gifts may go in a slightly—or completely—different direction from those of your spouse, or your parents, or your siblings, or your kids, but regardless of that, *you have them.*

This message is all about honoring those gifts within you and putting them to use in whatever way God wants. But you have to let God lead you. *That's* the main thing my health issues were telling me.

You may have a great idea that will provide the greatest

benefit humankind has ever seen since the discovery of fire. You may have a powerful, brilliant concept that will eradicate all the ills of humanity in one single swipe. It may even be a little crazy—so crazy that it consumes you as your life's work.

That's great. That's how I feel about what I'm doing. But what I'm discovering is that I have to be careful about it, because it's obviously messed with me to the point that I drove my own body into incapacitating illness and head-pounding discomfort. And all because I started believing something wrong.

I had been believing that the work I was doing was about the *work itself*. I would never have come out and said this or even really acknowledged this wayward thinking; but as I processed what my friend told me at that dinner, I began to realize and *really internalize* that *I* have nothing to do with it. In reality, the work done through XXXchurch or any of our other efforts isn't about what I do or about what any of our volunteers or other staff members do. It's all about what God wants to do *through* us—what He *can* do through us if we fully yield ourselves to His leading and calling.

Maybe, just maybe, people like me who want to work really hard and do stuff—maybe we just wind up getting in God's way.

I decided to take my friend's advice and decrease so that God can increase.

I had just gotten out of seminary and was twenty-two years old when I got my first ministry job as a youth pastor for a church near where I went to school. It had been my dream job since I was a wide-eyed kid in youth group, and I was beyond excited to have it. I relished the thought of pouring into these students and teaching them to develop a real relationship with Jesus.

After a short while of being a youth pastor, though, I hooked up with my friend Jake Larson, who was also a youth pastor at the time. We started doing some speaking and other ministry work on the side, traveling together to different summer camps, retreats, and conferences, still focusing mainly on students.

We called our little show *Craig and Jake LIVE*—which is a very, very Christian-in-the-'90s kind of title—and took it on the road to much acclaim. We were just two young, energetic guys who would go onstage in front of teenagers and tell stories from our lives, usually making fun of ourselves, but always bringing it back to Jesus and putting the focus on Him in some form or fashion.

*Craig and Jake LIVE* was a hit, and the more times we did it, the more momentum and traction we got. Plus, it was just great fun.

Jake and I had a good conversation one time, fairly early on in our tour, and said to each other, "We don't really want to be forty years old and saying to ourselves how we really enjoyed doing *Craig and Jake LIVE* for a little while, but then quit doing it because we got married and had kids and had to settle down and focus on our 'real' jobs."

In other words we had a vision for something more along the lines we were created for. Our personalities and gifts, we realized, lay outside the skill set of strictly doing student ministry while on staff at a local church. That is very important, life-changing work—and we weren't the right guys for it.

Instead we were discovering that our calling lay in speaking and traveling; we felt so much more alive and in the center of God's will when we were onstage during *Craig and Jake LIVE*. That was our element. So we talked it over, prayed about it, and eventually quit our youth pastor jobs, created a nonprofit organization we called Fireproof Ministries, and focused entirely on *Craig and Jake LIVE* for the time being. We didn't know if we would do that forever, but we knew that it was what we wanted to do for that moment in our lives.

I had only been married four months when we did that. It feels like a long time ago. But we did that for a good six years and spoke to hundreds of thousands of kids along the way. It was great.

XXXchurch was birthed out of *Craig and Jake LIVE*, with the help of another guy named Mike Foster. And when we decided to wind down *Craig and Jake LIVE* after six years, I began focusing full-time on XXXchurch, which is where my passions were more dedicated anyway.

Since then we've launched other ministries under the

umbrella of Fireproof, including XXXchurch, Strip Church, Nonprofitland, and iParent.tv. In case you're wondering, we had nothing to do with the Kirk Cameron movie *Fireproof.* That was the Kendrick Brothers from Sherwood Baptist Church in Georgia, though we do occasionally get letters in our post-office box from people who seem to think we have something to do with that film and who thank us for it, which is nice.

The point is, I spent almost fifteen years basically doing ministry nonstop. Rare was the month when I didn't have to travel somewhere or get involved in some big project or send out a bunch of e-mails to keep people on their toes as they did various things for our ministry. I never took any substantive time off. Never took a lengthy vacation or a sabbatical.

And then, suddenly, I started getting those headaches. Weird, huh?

In retrospect it all makes sense, but at the time I was actually a little terrified at the thought of slowing down and actually *going small.*

But I decided to do it. I *needed* to do it for my family, my wife and children, who were wondering out loud whether I was going to die. I needed to do it for my health. I needed to do it for my sanity.

I e-mailed Michelle, the person who handles all the booking for speaking engagements through XXXchurch, and told her I was going to take off that fall, and not to book me until the following year. You know what her response was? I'll quote her:

"That's the best news I've ever heard."

Part of her job is booking my speaking engagements, but she was excited that I was slowing down for a season and dialing everything back. Why? Because she's my friend and she cares about me.

I guess what I'm taking a long time to say is that this concept of going small is not the easiest thing in the world to grasp. Especially not for someone like me. I love hearing that God must increase, but the extra part of that—the part where I have to decrease—that part is pretty difficult.

But time off can help you understand how much of your faith is based on God and how much of it is based on your own self-importance. The fact is: *I needed to learn to decrease.* The idea of going small was just an idea until it became something I had to enact specifically in order to maintain my health.

God's promise is true: decreasing myself has allowed God to increase in ways I'd never imagined. He is indeed doing some great new things to grow us and allow us to spread into new avenues of reaching people with our message. By decreasing in my own world, I've given God an unprecedented opportunity to increase His presence in that same world of mine. To make me more aware of Him and to remind me of all He is capable of doing when I just get out of His way and let Him do His thing.

By decreasing, by going small, I can become more aware of Him.

I posted a short note on my website:

Over the last fifteen-plus years, I have spent a lot of time—perhaps too much—on the road: driving rental cars, sleeping in hotels, walking on and off airplanes. My family has been fortunate to travel with me all over the world. Sometimes I take them all, and other times I take one of the kids or someone on our staff with me.

I hate to fly but I love to get the message of XXXchurch out in front of people. However, this past summer, I have been dealing with some different health issues, none of which have been resolved as I write this. I have had several different tests on my heart, head, and brain, and as of right now, the results have been inconclusive and I have no answers.

The idea behind the book is that God delights in the small things and doesn't need us to chase just the big stuff. I thought the book was going to be a good book for people who are not wired like me, but I think I am learning what this means . . . and I'm going to take some time to rest and figure out what is going on.

My friend Jamie is on a sabbatical right now after spending seven years running his nonprofit. I am slightly jealous and would love to do something like that, but I also know it's not like me to just break away completely from something I love.

I just finished a lot of promotions and speaking for my new book *Open* and am going to be taking a break from speaking this fall. I have a few events I have already committed to (including two debates with Ron Jeremy, a couple of chapels for some football teams, a weekend in Green Bay and a TedX talk), so I'm going to do those.

We have a number of great speakers on our team. Hit up *michelle@fireproofministries.com* for 2014 dates and other options for the fall from our team.

I'm also going to take some time off, just to be home. I am still going to be working, but I'm going to try to let our team lead a bit more with me out of the way. I plan to help coach my daughter's soccer team, drive my son around on auditions, and sit on the sideline at his soccer games and work a little less than I have.

I won't have automatic e-mail replies that indicate I'm at the beach and not responding to e-mails for the rest of the year. My phone will still work, but I just might not respond to texts within seconds, and I might not call you back within the hour.

At the beginning of 37, I felt like I was just getting started, but now, toward the end of 37, I feel like my best days might be behind me. I know that's not true, but that's how it feels. I don't like the waiting, the not knowing, especially when it comes to my health. Slowing down will be a challenge, but I believe it's a challenge God is putting in front of me.

Are there areas of your life where you need to slow down? Where God is calling you to decrease so He can increase, and show you the miraculous world of the ordinary?

Interestingly, this manuscript was due to the publisher before I'll have genuinely started my intentional period of slowing down, so I can't tell you how it went. Because I don't yet know. I may hate it. I may love it.

I don't know how I'm going to handle this, but I do know that God is good, and He sees me, and He's going to honor whatever I do in His name, as long as I do it humbly and in grace, trusting that He'll take it wherever it needs to go.

And often, where it needs to go is small.

# NOTES

## Chapter 1

The story of the suicide note left at the Golden Gate Bridge comes from a *Newsweek* article called "The Suicide Epidemic" by Tony Dokoupil. It is well worth reading in its entirety, and can be accessed here: *http://www.thedailybeast.com/newsweek/2013/05/22/why-suicide-has-become-andepidemic-and-what-we-can-do-to-help.html*

The story about Clive Jacobsen, the prison pen-pal man, came from a video on YouTube called "Prison Pals: Meet the Man Who Writes to More Than 550 Prisoners (The Feed)," YouTube .com, uploaded by the user SBS2Australia on August 21, 2013, and which can be accessed here: *http://www.youtube.com/watch?v=WrHBMsEknx4*

## Chapter 2

"Everyone wants a revolution. No one wants to do the dishes." That line came from an excellent blog post by Tish Harrison Warren called *Courage in the Ordinary*, posted on April 3, 2013, at Intervarsity. You should read it, and you can access it here: *http://thewell.intervarsity.org/blog/courage-ordinary*

## Chapter 3

You can read about the advancement of the word *silly* in the Oxford English Dictionary. Specifically: "silly, adj., n., and adv," *OED Online*, accessed December 27, 2013, Oxford University Press, *http://0-www.oed.com.library.uark.edu/view/Entry/17976 1?rskey=j1XWvk&result=1&isAdvanced=false*

## Chapter 4

Thanks to our friend Isaiah for telling us about the Queen of the Night.

You can read about the adventures of Paul and Barnabas in Lystra in Acts 14:8–18.

## Chapter 5

If you try to market Blindness Removal Mud, you owe me a percentage of your profits.

## Chapter 6

I heard about the Underbelly Project from a friend, then read about it in Jasper Rees's article "Street Art Way Below the Street" in the *New York Times*, published on October 31, 2010. Since I didn't have a time machine to go back to 2010 and buy that particular issue of the paper, I looked it up online here: *http://www.nytimes.com/2010/11/01/arts/design/01underbelly .html?_r=1&*

*Exit Through the Gift Shop* was directed by Banksy in 2010 for Paranoid Pictures. It's rated "R" for a handful of swearwords, in case that bothers you.

The depressing truth of a man who can eat a lot of food in a little amount of time can be discovered in Ian Begley's "Joey Chestnut Eats 69 Hot Dogs," from ESPN.com on July 4, 2013. Here's the link, should you decide to uncover the truth

for yourself: *http://espn.go.com/espn/story/_/id/9450389/
joey-chestnut-downs-69-dogs-breakown-mark*

You'll want to read more about Rachel Beckwith's Charity:
Water campaign and its aftermath in this piece by
James Eng from NBC News from July 20, 2012, "Rachel's
Legacy: Year After Girl's Death, Mom Goes to Africa to
Honor Her Clean Water Wish," *http://usnews.nbcnews
.com/_news/2012/07/20/12835490-rachels-legacy-yearafter
-girls-death-mom-goes-to-africa-to-honor-her-clean-water
-wish?lite*

## Chapter 7

I encourage you to watch Jefferson's poem, "Why I Hate
Religion, But Love Jesus," here: *http://www.youtube.com/
watch?v=1IAhDGYlpqY*

Those PBS fake posters are kind of a subtle, subversive
work of art. You can view them all here: *http://insidetv
.ew.com/2013/05/28/pbs-fake-subway-ads/*

## Chapter 9

The portion of the epic saga of Abraham covered in this chapter
can be found in Genesis 15–18, roughly, with the story of Isaac's
birth told in Genesis 21.

## Chapter 10

The story of Vedran Smailovic, the Cellist of Sarajevo,
was brought to our attention through this blog post on
InternetMonk.com by Chaplain Mike: "For Memorial Day:
Another Look—Music of Peace in the Midst of Chaos," May 27,
2013, *http://www.internetmonk.com/archive/for-memorial-day-
another-look-music-ofpeace-in-the-midst-of-chaos*

Ingrid Loyau-Kennett's story was told in multiple news outlets.
Here's one where you can read more about it: Leo Hickman,

"Woolwich Attack Witness Ingrid Loyau-Kennett: 'I feel like a fraud,'" *The Guardian,* May 27, 2013, *http://www.guardian .co.uk/uk/2013/may/27/woolwich-witness-ingrid-loyaukennett*

## Chapter 13

You can find the Lord's Prayer in Matthew 6:9–13 or in Luke 11:2–4. Traditionally, most Christians add "for Yours is the kingdom, and the power, and the glory forever" to the end of it.

## Chapter 14

The Beastie Boys song in question is "Intergalactic," from the album *Hello Nasty* (Capitol Records, 1998).

# ABOUT THE AUTHOR

Craig Gross is an author, speaker, pastor, and revolutionary. He shot to prominence in 2002 when he founded the website XXXchurch.com as a response to the hurting he saw both in those addicted to pornography and those who made their living in the porn industry. In the 10 years since it began, XXXchurch.com has had over 70 million visitors to the website and his ministry is the subject of an award winning documentary.

Craig also spearheaded the development of X3watch, an internet accountability system that is used by over 1 million people. Craig is the author of nine books and has been featured in *GQ* magazine, *Newsweek, Time, Wired,* the *New York Times,* the *Los Angeles Times,* and has appeared on *Good Morning America, Nightline,* CNN, Fox News, and *The Daily Show with Jon Stewart.* He currently resides in Los Angeles, CA, with his wife, Jeanette, and their two children, Nolan and Elise.